The Genius of

generosity

Lessons from a secret pact
between two friends

CHIP INGRAM

Authors: Chip Ingram, with Chris Tiegreen
Editing by: Patrick Johnson and Steve Chapman, GenerousChurch
Proofreading by: Valerie Dyke
Cover and interior design by: Rule29 | rule29.com

Published in association with Yates & Yates, www.yates2.com

To order copies for your church,
visit GenerousChurch.com/Genius

Contents

Introduction

BY PATRICK JOHNSON,
CHIEF ARCHITECT OF GENEROUSCHURCH

The "secrets" to being financially savvy are all around us. Go to your local Barnes & Noble to read all the books written on how to manage your finances. Turn on the television to hear wise tips from financial experts. Surf the Internet to skim the "Seven Habits of Highly Successful Money Managers."

The truth is, most people want to be financially savvy.

And some say to be smart, you must spend carefully. Others say to be wise, you must save regularly. But as the title of this book reads, to be genius, you must give generously.

The first chapter of *Genius of Generosity* tells the story of John Saville and Chip Ingram: two men who came together to experience the genius of generosity. John possessed resources to give, and Chip lived among people with needs to be met. And their partnership in giving produced a unique joy and friendship that can teach us much in our own quest for financial intelligence ... and spiritual growth.

As you read, there are a number of unique features in each chapter to help you go deeper:

- **Bright Ideas** – Fresh, thought-provoking concepts about generosity

- **The Genius Life** – Examples of people (or communities) living out the genius of generosity in real life ... each with a web link that takes you to an online video version of the story

- **Discussion and Reflection** – Summaries and reflection questions about the Bright Ideas, stories, and content from the chapter ... designed to help guide your personal reflection or small group discussion

After reading Chapter One, be sure to read the "Take Action: The Genius Giving Group" section at the end of the book. The greatest way to learn the genius of generosity is to practice it in real time with others. So we encourage you to form a "Genius Giving Group" with your small group, family, or friends and then find someone in need right around you who you can bless by giving your money, your time, and your life.

And then compare your experience with the lessons learned by John and Chip – and watch your generosity IQ skyrocket!

Chapter 1
WHY IT'S GENIUS
TO BE GENEROUS

'm not sure where I got the idea, but until my mid-20s, I thought
generosity was something reserved for people who were either very rich
or very holy. Growing up in a middle class family in central Ohio, I knew
I was neither.

Now don't get me wrong. I knew that being selfish was completely
unacceptable. But generosity in my young mind was reserved for another
day—like when I win the lottery or make it to the major leagues or own
my own business. Sharing, kindness, being fair, and appearing relatively
generous were all values I embraced and sought to practice, but genuine,
open-handed, even lavish generosity was something for the rich and the
ultra-virtuous.

In my mind, generosity required a lot of things I knew I didn't have, like a
big bank account and an even bigger heart for God and others. Generosity
seemed like a characteristic you might try to develop someday when the
chips fall your way and you have some extra to spread around. It was like
Christianity's grad school. Besides, I was having a pretty hard time just

making ends meet. I thought of the Christian life as a bit like being in the military in those days. I joined the army of God to fulfill a mission as day by day I sought to follow Christ. To me, generosity was reserved for "the few, the proud, the Marines." It might be a great thing to aspire to, but certainly not something within the grasp of a very ordinary Christ-follower like myself.

But that all changed when I met a man named John Saville. I would learn then that generosity has little or nothing to do with how much money you have or how far along you perceive yourself to be on your spiritual journey. In fact, I was shocked to learn that being generous has much more to do with being smart, shrewd, wise, and deliriously happy. In a word, I discovered that generosity is genius!

JOHN SAVILLE AND THE SECRET PACT

I met John in the first church I pastored in rural Texas. I was a young, inexperienced pastor with a lot of zeal and not much wisdom. John, by contrast, was an elderly man who came to Christ late in life and had suffered some pretty hard knocks along the way. We had absolutely nothing in common except that he was the chairman of the elders and I was the new pastor of this not-so-thriving church of 35 people in a town of 3,500.

To be candid, I thought John was a little kooky at first. He had simple answers for my "complex" questions; he quoted Galatians 2:20 or Oswald Chambers as the answer to almost everything. On top of that, he said "praise the Lord" a lot, which was very uncool in my mind. And he drove a Cadillac, which caused me to question his spiritual maturity. I mean, how can you really love God and have nice stuff? That didn't make sense to me.

John wasn't up on sports, pop culture, or church growth. I was in my late 20s, and he was in his mid 70s. There was absolutely no reason for John and I to see each other except for a once a month elders meeting, let alone become best friends—apart from the genius of generosity.

One day John asked me drive into Dallas to have lunch with him at the downtown accounting firm he owned. He told me to wear a tie because the restaurant required it. I'll never forget how intimidated I was as I traveled up the glass building's elevator to his wood-paneled reception area. My middle-class roots were being deeply challenged as we dined on the top floor overlooking all of Dallas. It was a world I had never experienced, and John seemed particularly thrilled to treat me to the best he could offer and insist that I get the filet—"best steak around," he assured me.

Toward the end of lunch, this grand old man pulled a small white box from his coat pocket and told me he had a proposition that he wanted me to consider. He called it a business deal of sorts. Not a business deal to make money, but a business deal to give it away. I will never forget John's three-point outline as he laid out what he called our "Secret Pact":

1. I have a desire to help poor and hurting people.
2. You are in contact with poor and hurting people daily.
3. I want you to be my eyes and ears and help them as God leads you.

With that, John reached into the box, pulled out a brown checkbook, and handed it to me. As I opened it, I saw the words "pastor's discretionary fund" neatly printed on the front. The deposit ledger in the back had a five and three zeros neatly printed in the far right column. I looked up at this loving, kooky man and said, "Do you mean you want me to figure out who to help and then help them the way you would if you saw the situation, Mr. Saville?"

John smiled and said, "That's exactly what I want you to do Chip!"

Five thousand dollars, five thousand dollars … My head was swimming as I repeated that number over and over riding down the elevator to get in my old non-air-conditioned-car in the 98-degree Dallas summer heat. John had sworn me to secrecy, and thus began a series of divine lessons that only later would I recognize as the genius of generosity.

AN UNEXPECTED ADVENTURE

John's idea was intriguing, and the cause was inspiring. But I was a little overwhelmed at first. What if I chose to give to the wrong people or for the wrong reasons? How much should I give in each situation? How would I figure out which cases were legitimate and which ones weren't? It felt like a lot of pressure, and I was nervous. But over time, it got easier and it got to be fun. Each day as I prepared to leave the house, I put my wallet in one back pocket and John's checkbook in the other. I started to feel like Santa Claus every day of the year, wondering who God wanted to help with John's money. It turned into an exciting adventure.

Three things happened in my life as a result of this deal, and all of them had major impact. First, rarely a day went by that I didn't think about John Saville. Whenever I encountered someone in need—a young girl dealing with an unplanned pregnancy and preparing for a baby, or a family at church whose funds had completely run dry—I had to try to see through John's eyes. I was constantly asking myself, "What would John do in this situation? How would he spend his money here?"

> Three things happened in my life as a result of this deal, and all of them had major impact.

John and I had known each other for over a year because of our roles at church, but our paths only crossed once a week at church. I had rarely spent time thinking about John— until our deal. Then, I found myself thinking about him multiple times a day, wondering how he would feel about certain situations and how he would respond to them. Over the next few months, I felt a lot closer to him than I ever had.

The second thing that happened was that I quickly learned how to balance a checkbook. I had never been particularly careful about my own. In fact, when I first got married, my idea of balancing a checkbook was to have a pretty close estimate of what the bank said I had. I didn't have much, so that wasn't really a problem. My wife had to explain that coming up with a sum that was within $20 or $30 of the bank's figures wasn't good enough. But that was with my money. Now that I was handling John's money, I had to be ready for him to ask me how things were going. I would have to give an account. There was no way I could face him if I had gotten a couple hundred dollars off track over time. I learned how to be faithful pretty quickly.

Third, John and I became great friends. He never made me feel like his errand boy. Every few months, he would invite me into Dallas for lunch—and not the kind of lunch I was used to. This was no fast-food combo meal or daily special at the local diner. This was a celebration.

So I would meet John at his office, and we would take the elevator up to the top floor of his skyscraper where you could see all of Dallas while you ate. The restaurant staff would greet him by name and give us menus with no prices on them. Waiters with white towels over their arms would come take our order and meet every need down to the tiniest details. And John would prompt me to indulge: "The filet is great here. Want to try it—and maybe some lobster with it?" He would remind me that God had been good to him and that he wanted to give me the best lunch possible. We were there to celebrate. So three or four times a year, John would buy me an extravagant meal and I would tell him extravagant stories of how God had used his money.

After we got through talking about the pregnant teenagers and unemployed families and unpaid medical bills and down-and-outers who needed a helping hand—story after story after story—John would utter an uncomfortably loud "praise the Lord" and then, with a twinkle in his eye, say, "Let's do it again!" And he would fill up the discretionary account with some more funds and we'd start the cycle all over again. It was one of the wildest experiences I've ever had.

Do you see what happened? This "deal" or partnership, as he put it, caused me to get to know John, learn his perspective, and gain unique insight about how he wanted me to spend his money. It caused me to become very faithful and accountable in what he had entrusted to me. And it caused this old godly man and young energetic pastor who had little in common to become best friends as we celebrated the fruits of our efforts.

I'm sure you see the spiritual correlation by now. This is a pretty powerful picture of our relationship with God and the way we manage His resources. Why did I start thinking about John all the time? Because I had a responsibility to act in his interests—just as God invites us to represent Him in this world. Why did I become faithful? Because it was his money—just as we become faithful stewards of the resources God entrusts to us. Why did John and I become such good friends? Because we got together to celebrate—just as God enjoys celebrating with us over the fruit He bears through us when we partner with Him to love those in need.

A BRILLIANT WAY TO LIVE

You'll notice that there was nothing obligatory about this arrangement between John and me. Sure, John had some authority as a senior elder of the church, and maybe that influenced me somewhat at first. But I knew I didn't have to accept his deal. I wanted to. And over time, any hint of obligation got lost in the joy of the journey. You'll also notice that neither one of us felt self-righteous about it, as though we were trying to impress someone. There was no sacrificial martyrdom or painful "oughts" or "shoulds" or guilt-trips. No, these were great adventures followed by great celebrations.

That's God's design for the way we give and express His generosity. Giving is meant to be joyful and fulfilling. It isn't rooted in guilt, self-righteousness, or a martyr complex. It's rooted in joy. And, in fact, it's genius. It's the smartest way to live.

Let me explain what I mean by the "genius of generosity." I've chosen those words for a reason. "Genius" comes from a Latin word meaning "to produce" and represents quality and natural ability. We use it for anyone with a really high IQ. In other words, it describes someone with brilliant intellect and skills. In Hebrew, the word "generosity" literally means to saturate with water, a symbol of life—to overflow in a way that brings life to people. In Greek, it means "ready to distribute"—available to give time, talent, and treasure to bless others. When you put all of these connotations together, you start to get a dramatic picture. My point in pairing these words is to emphasize that generosity—a life overflowing with care and concern for others—is a brilliant way to live. It isn't supposed to be a high, noble, sacrificial calling for a few super-spiritual people. Spending and saving carefully are wise, but giving generously is genius. Both practically and spiritually, it's one of the smartest, most intellectually sound and emotionally satisfying decisions you will ever make for your life now and forever.

Bright Idea

To be smart, spend carefully. To be wise, save regularly. To be genius, give extravagantly.

GENEROSITY WORKS

Maybe you're used to thinking of generosity as a "have-to"—a necessary but unappealing aspect of the Christian life. If so, let's take a look at four simple reasons why it's really the most intelligent way to live.

1. Generosity is genius because it changes our lives.

That's about as pragmatic as I can get. Generosity works. People who give generously feel great about it and find themselves blessed in ways they never expected. Great things happen in them, and great things happen to those around them. It's the ultimate win-win situation.

We know this is true first and foremost because it's Biblical. Jesus said it is more blessed to give than to receive (Acts 20:35). And Proverbs 11:25 tells us, "A generous man will prosper; he who refreshes others will himself be refreshed." The word for "prosper" literally implies that generous people will be "fat"—not that they will need a good diet plan, but that they will overflow with abundance. Proverbs, a book full of God-given wisdom for life, advises us that if we want the quality of life that will be fulfilling to us and pleasing to God, we will be generous.

There's plenty of evidence to prove this truth even if it wasn't in the Bible. Simple observation shows us clearly that people who behave in a miserly, greedy, selfish way are miserable. There's a reason Ebenezer Scrooge is no one's role model; he had plenty of money but no fulfilling relationships and no joy. There's a reason so many lottery winners talk about how their winning ticket ruined their life; it changed their perspective and their relationships. And there's a reason so many families are divided when they have to sort out a rich relative's will; the greed and selfishness cultivate anger, bitterness, and depression. A stingy heart ends up empty.

2. Generosity connects us with others.

When people are generous and gracious, they exude love and happiness. There's something very attractive about those who have a sense of kindness, who do nice things for others, who pick up a bill or go out of their way to do a favor. Generous people create positive feelings in their relationships. They cause others to want to be around them.

We get a lift when we give, don't we? Whenever we go out of our way to help or encourage someone, we feel encouraged and positive. Something happens inside. It's good for us and good for others.

I vividly remember experiencing this a number of years ago at a coffee shop where I would go regularly to study. I got to know many of the people who would come in early in the morning, but there was one guy who never communicated. He was a homeless man who looked like he had done some hard drugs and had some deep scars. No smile, no wave, no eye contact.

He would get a cup of coffee and just sit there in a stupor.

I started to wonder what this guy's story was and felt a prompting to find out—or at least to help him out a little. "Excuse me," I said. "Could I buy you another cup of coffee?" He shook his head. "No, seriously—what are you drinking?" I asked.

He told me, so I got him a cup and returned to my table to study. After about an hour, I got up to go to the bathroom, and when I came back, he looked up at me. "Did you see the sunrise this morning?" he asked.

"No," I said.

"Come here. Look out this window."

I went over and looked at the pink sky.

"Do you see those two lights there?" he asked. "See the real bright one? That's Venus. The one next to it is Mars. They're only gonna show like this for four days."

> When people are generous and gracious, they exude love and happiness.

"You're kidding," I said. He explained all kinds of things I hadn't known anything about.

I went back the next morning, and Mike—I learned his name—gave me a big smile. "Look at this," he said. The sun wasn't quite up yet, and Venus and Mars were glowing brightly. I called the other guys over and showed them what Mike had shown me. We all stood there and looked at this awesome scene.

After that, Mike and I would talk with each other about our lives. He was a construction worker—a bright, talented guy who had been through some really hard times. I got to hear his stories and experience a new friendship all because I was willing to spend a buck and a half for coffee and take some time to show that I cared about him. Even that little bit of generosity opened up a fascinating door.

3. Generosity helps us invest in what matters.

Generosity is also genius because it's a guaranteed, high-yield investment. This is more than just a pragmatic issue. Spiritually, generosity protects us from short-sighted, bad investments of our time, our talent, and our treasure and creates long-term wealth.

In a sense, everything you do is an investment. You are always pouring your time, talent, and treasure into something. And whatever you're pouring into, that's where your heart is. You devote yourself to certain people, projects, and possessions. It's unavoidable. You can do that intentionally, or you can do it randomly. Either way, you're constantly making an investment. And every investment has its returns, either for good or for bad. Scripture describes this as "sowing and reaping"; whatever we sow now, that's what we'll reap later. And Jesus spoke about this principle in His sermon on the mount. If you want to be protected from bad investments and avoid their devastating consequences down the road, generosity will do that for you. Here's what Jesus said:

"Do not store up for yourselves treasures on earth, where moth and rust destroy, and where thieves break in and steal. But store up for yourselves treasures in heaven, where moth and rust do not destroy, and where thieves do not break in and steal. For where your treasure is, there your heart will be also. The eye is the lamp of the body. If your eyes are good, your whole body will be full of light. But if your eyes are bad, your whole body will be full of darkness. If then the light within you is darkness, how great is that darkness! No one can serve two masters. Either he will hate the one and love the other, or he will be devoted to the one and despise the other. You cannot serve both God and Money" (Matthew 6:19-24).

This begins with a negative command: literally, "stop storing up for yourselves treasure on earth." Does that mean it's wrong to save or invest, to plan for the future, or to enjoy something nice? No, it can't mean that; there are other verses in the Bible that tell us to save, invest, plan, and enjoy. The key to understanding this command is the phrase "for yourselves," and it points to greed, self-interest, pleasure-seeking, hoarding, and living only for the here and now. Jesus warns us not to live that way.

Why does Jesus give such a negative prohibition? It isn't because He's down on us but because He has our best in mind. In the first century, people accumulated wealth by storing up fine clothing, essential grains, and precious metals. And Jesus pointed out that every investment could be lost. Linens could be damaged by moths, crops could be destroyed, metals could rust, and thieves could steal any of the above. And while we don't necessarily accumulate wealth that way anymore—and we normally don't try to store it in our homes—savings and investments can be lost just as easily today. Bank assets and stock markets rise and fall. Nothing is perfectly secure; it's all vulnerable.

Jesus wants to protect us from such vulnerability. Whenever we put our focus entirely on gaining wealth and property and establishing our own needs and security, we aren't being very wise. It isn't smart to stake so much on uncertain things.

But Jesus followed up the negative command with a positive instruction: start storing up for yourselves treasure in heaven. Did you notice why? Because treasures can't be destroyed there. And did you notice who we're doing it for? Ourselves. You see, this isn't about self-sacrificial martyrdom. The motivation in this passage is our own best interests. We are told to store up treasures in heaven because if we really saw the big picture, that's what we would choose to do for ourselves. In the long run, that will benefit us more than any other choice.

Think about it. If eternity is an infinite timeline, all of human history could be represented by an inch. And within that inch, our own lives could be represented by a tiny dot. Jesus is telling us that in light of what He knows about eternity, we can allocate our treasures in a way that benefits us not only in the here and now (the tiny dot) but forever. In other words, we can leverage this minuscule slice of time we inhabit and the material things we have and turn them into eternal investments with lasting impact. That's an unbeatable return on investment!

So how do we store up treasure in heaven? There are a lot of ways to do that, but I'll give you three that are clearly spelled out in Scripture. One is by giving to the work of the Gospel—helping God's Word go out, bring people to Christ, and change their lives. Their lives are eternal.

We are told to store up treasures in heaven because if we really saw the big picture, that's what we would choose to do for ourselves.

We will see them in heaven, and they will know we helped make it possible for them to be there. Second, Jesus promised that every act of kindness, even as small as giving someone a cup of cold water in His name, will receive a reward in heaven. And third, when we give to the poor, we are literally lending to the Lord. He will repay us not only now but in eternity.

4. Generosity frees our hearts.

As we've just seen, Jesus told us what to do and what not to do with our money. He wanted to protect us from bad investments and set us up for everlasting ones. And this is about something far more important than our finances; it's a heart issue. The command is followed by a spiritual reason: "Where your treasure is, there your heart will be also."

Money is the mirror of our heart before God. If you want an accurate measure of your relationship with God, take a look at your checkbook and your credit card statements. Notice where your money is going. That will tell you what you're devoted to. And not only does the direction of your resources reflect where your heart is, it helps determine where your heart goes. Your heart will always follow your investments.

Bright Idea
Where your money goes, your heart flows.

Jesus went on to talk about your eyes as the lamp of the body. His point was that where you go and what you do—your decisions, opinions, and actions—are directed by what you see and how you see it. If your eye is good—literally, if it's "single"—you'll be full of light. You'll have undivided loyalty. The idea is that if you are single-mindedly focused on God and His kingdom, you will become liberal and generous with your resources. But if your eye is bad, your focus becomes selfish and greedy. In a Jewish expression of Jesus' time, an "evil eye" referred to someone who was miserly and selfish. That kind of life is full of darkness.

There are two kinds of treasures in life: those that are temporal and those that last forever. And we have to decide which kind we are going to live for—whether we are going to live for now or for eternity. If our eyes are on the things of God, He's our master. If our eyes are on the things of the world, then it's our master. And Jesus assures us that no one can serve two masters. No slave can follow the commands of different owners. We will have to choose one master and reject the other. If you want to find out who your master is, it's pretty simple: follow the money trail. It will show you where your heart is.

When we understand what life is really about—relationships, joy, and eternal impact—we reassess our investments and place them in what truly is a treasure. We evaluate all of our temporal possessions and arrange them in a way that maximizes the benefit to ourselves and others. We invest in what will bring us the greatest return on our investment—not because we're more righteous, more noble, or more spiritual than others, but because we're smarter.

IT ISN'T EASY BEING GENIUS

If living generously is so smart, why isn't everyone doing it? Because it's difficult. You would think everyone would see the wisdom in making investments that have eternal returns and such positive, practical payoff, but it isn't that simple. One of the reasons for that is the deceptive power of riches. Jesus told a parable about a sower who scattered his seeds into four different types of soil. Some of those seeds grew up among thorns and were unfruitful. The seed represented the Word of God, and the soil represented the spiritual condition of those who heard it. Jesus explained what the thorns symbolized: "the worries of this life, the deceitfulness of wealth and the desires for other things." When the truth of God's Word is planted in someone's heart, wealth and worldly worries can bend it and choke it and render it ineffective. Wealth is not neutral. It is powerful and deceptive. It can seduce even the most sincere Christ-follower and convince you that giving yourself, your time, and your money in love and generosity is too big of a risk.

Another reason many people don't see the benefits of a generous life is the lure of Mammon worship. That's what Jesus called it when He said no one could worship God and money. The word He used for money is "Mammon"—the false god of wealth. Money can take absolute control of our lives. It promises success, power, fame, status, security, control, and whatever else we want to buy. It says, "You can have it all, and you can have it now."

And it demands sacrifices too. Some people bow down to the shrine of success. I once had a conversation with a Silicon Valley executive who told me that when Forbes came out with its list of the 50 wealthiest people, number 51 wrote an eight-page letter explaining why he should have been on the list. For this person (and many of us), wealth is seen as the ticket to significance, power, and prestige. Unfortunately, it cultivates an ego-driven need to compare oneself with others. The game never ends and "enough" is never enough, no matter how much one accumulates. That's a high price to pay.

Others bow down to the shrine of security. If they hoard enough, they think they will be safe. Some flaunt their wealth for everyone to see. Who can have the biggest, most extravagant wedding, car, house, vacation, and toys? Who can live in the most impressive zip code? It's a never-ending competition. Others worship by always having to pick up the bill; it may seem generous at first, but it's often a means to make everyone indebted and control relationships. Mammon makes enormous promises that it never fulfills. It ends up only being a harsh taskmaster, destroying relationships and keeping its servants chasing after the wind.

Finally, it's so difficult to be generous because of what I call "temporal myopia"—nearsightedness. A man in a crowd once asked Jesus to settle an inheritance dispute between him and his brother. In response, Jesus warned the crowd to be on guard against all kinds of greed. "A man's life does not consist of the abundance of his possessions," He said (Luke 12:15). He then told a parable about a rich man who wanted to build bigger and bigger barns to store all his grain and goods. Then, the man told himself, he would take it easy—just eat, drink, and be merry. God called the man a fool. "This very night your life will be demanded from you. Then who will get what you have prepared for yourself?" Jesus said, "This is how it will be with anyone who stores up things for himself but is not rich toward God" (Luke 12:16-21).

That's temporal myopia. It's an illusion to think that we can arrive at a place where we don't have to work anymore but can only feed ourselves with pleasure. But millions chase after it, and it prevents them from living generously. What Mammon promises—security, significance, purpose, and happiness—only God can provide.

THE GATEWAY TO INTIMACY

The greatest treasure we could ever have is intimacy with God, and every obstacle to a generous lifestyle wars against it. In fact, generosity is a gateway into intimacy with Him. My relationship with John Saville was a picture of how jointly managing resources creates a bond between people. As I made decisions about John's money, I had to learn more about his desires. I had to get in touch with his heartbeat. I began to think like him and see through his eyes. And he had to show confidence in me, which increased as I became a good steward of what he had given. His trust in me became stronger over time. As we shared this endeavor—and as we shared the joy of its fruitfulness—we developed a close friendship and a deep bond.

Bright Idea
Generosity is a gateway into intimacy with God.

That's how it is with God. Our stewardship of His resources isn't just an assignment. It's relational. As we seek His will and make decisions about His gifts, we grow closer to Him. We begin to see through His eyes and develop His heartbeat. He entrusts us with more and more, and together we celebrate the fruitfulness that comes out of this relationship. Our generosity is a gateway into intimacy with Him.

Do you see the irony? We get our greatest treasure by giving and sharing rather than hoarding and accumulating. When we let go of the temporal and quit focusing on ourselves, and when we embrace instead the eternal treasures He offers us by investing in Kingdom-oriented relationships and purposes, we get rich. By releasing more of what we have, we receive more than we could ever imagine. It's a counter-intuitive but brilliant way to live. It really is genius.

WHAT TO EXPECT

The rest of this book will explore how we can become the brilliant people we were meant to be—those who understand and benefit from the genius of generosity. We'll explore God's design for giving and how He intends to bless those who become living expressions of His generous heart. We'll see that the first steps on the road to genius include giving the first and best of our resources in a regular systematic way; that giving generously and in increasing proportion requires great faith; and that the heart of true generosity is a heart of sacrifice and worship. In this journey, we'll explore how God's wisdom goes so much deeper than human reasoning—and how an investment in His ways leads to greater fulfillment and joy than most people ever experience.

THE GENIUS LIFE: BILL AND VONETTE BRIGHT
A couple's contract with God

In 1951, a young couple in Los Angeles decided to sign a contract surrendering everything they owned to Jesus. A few years earlier, the husband had been a businessman focused on trying to build his own empire. But coming to Christ had changed his perspective, and he and his wife began to think about what they really wanted out of life. So they wrote out a contract with God.

The contract reflected a decision to no longer work day and night for the bottom line—that instead of building their business to lay up treasures on earth, they would trust God and lay up treasures in heaven. One day later, God gave them a vision for the world that would change millions of lives. And Campus Crusade for Christ was born.

"Everything about you is influenced by your view of God," Bill said. "That's the reason we've never felt we should take a penny. We're not our own, we've been bought with a price, the precious blood of the Lord Jesus."

Bill and Vonette Bright didn't just offer their income to God; they offered every area of their lives—"total, absolute, irrevocable surrender," Bill said shortly before his death in 2003. Millions of dollars would pass through their hands, but they gave all of it away except for their modest annual salary. They made a decision not to accept royalties for books or honorariums for speaking engagements. They gave away their pension to start a campus center at a Russian university. Even a $1 million grant that came with the Templeton Prize for Progress in Religion in 1996 was quickly put to use for kingdom purposes. They insisted that they had already given everything away in 1951.

The Brights knew when they started their ministry that God would lead them and provide everything they needed. They found the well-known statement true: "You can't out-give God."

That perspective shaped a global ministry that has impacted college campuses and nations for decades. The Brights built their lives on the belief that if you use whatever you have for God's glory, He takes care of everything else. And using it for God's glory means fulfilling the Great Commission. The Brights emphasized that when we get to heaven, the issue won't be how much money we made; it will be whether we were faithful to what He called us to do.

"Your view of God determines everything—your lifestyle, friends, literature, the music you enjoy," Bill said. "Everything about you is influenced by your view of God. That's the reason we've never felt we should take a penny. We're not our own, we've been bought with a price, the precious blood of the Lord Jesus."

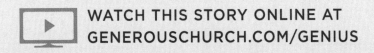 **WATCH THIS STORY ONLINE AT GENEROUSCHURCH.COM/GENIUS**

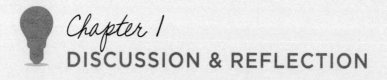

Chapter 1
DISCUSSION & REFLECTION

The following is a summary of the ideas and questions from Chapter 1. Use them for personal reflection or small group discussion, and consider journaling to record your thoughts and impressions.

BRIGHT IDEAS

Which of these "Bright Ideas" has the most meaning for you? Why?

- To be smart, spend carefully. To be wise, save regularly. To be genius, give extravagantly.

- Where your money goes, your heart flows.

- Generosity is a gateway into intimacy with God.

IMPACT FROM THE BILL AND VONETTE BRIGHT STORY

What aspects of the Brights' lives were involved in their contract with God? In what ways did the Brights honor that contract? In what ways did God?

Does the Brights' story inspire you to make any commitments toward God? If so, what?

REFLECTION QUESTIONS

1   When you were growing up, how would you describe your family's view toward money? What was your family's attitude toward generosity?

2   Who is the most generous person you know? Who has blessed you by their generosity?

3   How would you describe where you are today on the journey toward generosity? How big of a priority is it for you and what are some barriers to being more generous?

4   Chip said "Generosity works." Brainstorm a list of ways that generosity makes for a richer, better life. How has this principle of "generosity works" played itself out in your life?

5   If we were to look at your life in the past, where have you been tempted to follow the world's thinking about money? Are you tempted to believe and behave as though money will bring security, significance, purpose, or happiness?

Chapter 2
THE PRINCIPLE
WITH SECRET POWER

Early in my life as a Christian, somewhere between college and seminary, I was a teacher making about $1,000 a month and had very few expenses. I had been discipled by some people who did a good job of teaching me the basics—how to have a quiet time, memorize verses, share my faith, and give the first portion of my income to God. I didn't necessarily have the right perspective on money, but I knew how to be obedient and tithe. The Christians who taught me about giving weren't legalistic about it. They considered 10 percent, give or take a percentage point, to be a good start—a minimum commitment—but weren't rigid about it. So that's where my giving journey started.

I paid about $120 in rent, so I had quite a bit of my monthly income left over. I decided I would increase my percentage of giving to 20 percent, then 30. And I have to confess, I was a little pharisaical about it. Somehow I got the idea that the more I gave, the more spiritual I would be and the more God would love me. And I was pretty proud of my percentage. Granted, 30 percent of a thousand dollars isn't very much, but I was impressed with my generosity. I even let it slip every once in a while so other people would be impressed too. I still didn't understand that it was all God's. I thought I was doing God a pretty big favor.

I owned a little green Volkswagen during this time. It was my first car, and it was pretty cool. I didn't know much about taking care of a car, but I kept it shiny and bright and put oil in it when it needed some. It ran great.

After I married Theresa and we decided to move to Dallas for me to attend seminary, we had to figure out what to do with our cars. We could only take one, and she had recently bought a nice Chevy Nova. It made sense to take hers with us and sell my Volkswagen. So I started thinking how much I'd be able to get for my car.

A Volkswagen of that model, year, and condition was going for about $600. But I kept thinking I could get more for it. Maybe $800. Perhaps even $1,000, as a gas shortage at the time was making cars like mine more valuable every day. The dollar signs kept increasing in my own mind—until I was driving to my teaching and coaching job one morning and heard a still, small voice.

"Chip, whose car is this?" The voice was still and small enough that I could ignore it. Surely that couldn't be God. I shifted my thoughts to the basketball practice I'd be leading later that day.

The voice came back the next day, and again the next. "Chip, whose car is this?" I've realized over the years that when you get a strong impression over and over again, and it lines up with Scripture and has something to do with serving and loving other people, it's probably the Holy Spirit. But it took me a while to figure that out back then. After about four days of denial, I answered.

"This is Your car, Lord," I said.

"That's right, Chip. I have a plan for this car." I would realize later that He really had a plan for my heart, not just the car.

"So what's Your plan for this car?" I asked.

"You know Nancy—your friend who's planning to be a Wycliffe missionary?"

"Yes."

"You have two cars, right?"

"Yes."

"She has no car, right?"

"Yes." I didn't like where this was going.

"She's moving to Southeast Asia to translate the Bible for a remote people group, she'll need to travel all over the United States to raise money and prayer support, and she'll need to drive something that doesn't use a lot of gas. I want you to take that car of mine—the one I've let you use for six years—and give it to her."

"You're kidding," I said. He wasn't kidding, of course, and I did what He said. Well, I eventually did what He said. First I tried to take my prized stereo out of the car before I gave it to her. Theresa came out to the garage while I was pulling it out.

"What are you doing?" she asked.

"Well, you know, honey … God said the car, but I mean … my stereo too?"

She just put her hands on her hips and gave me a look.

"Okay," I mumbled, and put the stereo back in.

I learned a lot from this incident, and I reluctantly obeyed God. But please understand: I didn't do it because I was naturally generous, noble, or godly. I did it simply because God said to. It was an obedience issue. And I learned an invaluable lesson—that I hadn't believed that everything I had really belonged to God. Even though I had been giving between 20 and 30 percent of my income, I had been doing it as a Pharisee in order to impress myself, others, and God. I still hadn't made it to first base in my understanding of stewardship, let alone the genius of generosity.

A NEW LENS OF STEWARDSHIP

Generosity is a beautiful word, isn't it? It flows from the tongue easily and conjures up images of joyful, extravagant giving and receiving. Stewardship, on the other hand, has a heavier, more serious tone for many people—one of obligation and strict limits on spending. But that's because Christians and many other groups have historically described stewardship in those narrow terms. On the contrary, Biblical stewardship is a truly beautiful thing. Why? Because it's an amazing privilege that God has given especially to us.

Remember my experience with John Saville? What was I to him? His steward, of course. And it was wonderful to play that role! It was an exciting adventure to give away the $5,000 to those in need around me. Instead of it feeling like a chore or boring obligation, it was a thrilling honor. Though it was challenging at times to make wise decisions that would faithfully represent John's wishes, writing those checks was one of the most joyful experiences I'd had in my entire life.

Even more exciting is the fact that everyone has this same opportunity. We are all God's stewards. And stewardship is a key part of why generosity is so genius. True generosity flows out of an understanding that God owns everything. In His economy, good stewardship is by nature generous and joyful; it directs His resources extravagantly toward His purposes and for His people to deeply enjoy. If we want to understand generosity biblically, we need to see stewardship through new lenses—less as a reluctant obligation and more as a thrilling opportunity.

> We need to see stewardship through new lenses—less as a reluctant obligation and more as a thrilling opportunity.

I know this is old news for many Christians. The Bible makes it clear that God owns everything—that however much we give back to Him financially, the rest still belongs to Him too. We are supposed to be stewards over everything He has entrusted to us, not just a certain percentage of it. But even though we have been taught that truth and intellectually accept it, most of us do not live as though we believe it's true. And more than that, we don't seem to understand why God entrusts us with His resources and calls us to manage them well. This isn't just a spiritual exercise or a test of obedience. There's a bigger purpose behind it.

Bright Idea

Stewardship is the path. Generosity is the adventure.

It's one thing to believe everything we have and everything we are belongs to God. It's another for that truth to sink down into our hearts where we feel it and grasp it. And when it really sinks down, all the way into our gut where it shapes everything we think and feel and do, our lives are transformed. We shift from simply having theoretical knowledge to being practical geniuses. We move from duty to delight; from rules we keep to an adventure we share. We wake up in the morning wondering what we are going to do with God's time or how we are going to spend His money. We think about how we are going to relate to the spouse and kids He entrusted to us or the friends He's placed in our lives. This powerful shift in perspective revolutionizes our relationship with God.

I call this "the oikonomia principle." Oikonomia is the Greek word from which we get "economy," but it literally means "household management." The principle is this: all that we are and all that we have belongs to God, and He has temporarily entrusted it to us to oversee according to His wishes. We are managers over God's household business.

We get a great picture of this in the Old Testament story of Joseph. Joseph was sold into slavery by his brothers and ended up in the household of an Egyptian officer named Potiphar. Potiphar made Joseph the steward of all his household responsibilities—the property management, the housework, the finances, the laborers, the cultivation of the land, etc. He put Joseph in charge and gave him power of attorney. Joseph ran the home, kept good accounts, and reported to his boss.

This concept shows up again and again in the Bible.

Our time Psalm 90:12 tells us that our time isn't actually ours but is entrusted to us.

Our spouse Proverbs 19:14 reminds us that our spouse comes from the Lord.

Our property Luke 16:12 says that we are to be trustworthy with the property given to us.

Our spiritual gifts Romans 12:6 indicates that we receive spiritual gifts by God's grace.

God's truth 1 Corinthians 4:1 calls us servants who have been entrusted with truth, the "secret things of God."

Our body Even our own body, according to 1 Corinthians 6:19-20, doesn't belong to us; we were bought at a price.

Everything we have and everything we are has been given to us.

The point I want to emphasize with this principle is not the fact that God owns everything and we're His stewards. Everyone who has been around Bible teaching for any length of time probably understands that. The deeper issue is trust—a relational issue. It's required of a steward that one be found trustworthy. God has entrusted to us everything we have for a reason—so we can partner with Him to accomplish His purposes, and so we can demonstrate where our true priorities lie.

This is why Jesus talked about money so often. It wasn't because God is in need of our money and Jesus wanted to make sure we gave it to Him. It was because the way we handle money is one of the most accurate reflections of our relationship with Him—and specifically our trustworthiness as His stewards.

CAN GOD TRUST YOU?

Jesus' provocative teaching about how to be a faithful steward is found in Luke 16—and, strangely, the main character of His story was a man who was dishonest with his master's money. The audience for this parable was not only Jesus' disciples but also the Pharisees who were scrutinizing His teachings. Over the years, many of them had taken a solid Old Testament teaching—that when God's people were living in a theocracy and were obedient to Him, He would bless them materially—and twisted it into a justification for making themselves rich through dishonesty and a corrupt religious system. They sought wealth, even through injustice, so people would assume they were righteous and blessed by God. Their view of material wealth was misguided. They had it backwards; they were leveraging long-term values for short-term gain. So Jesus told a parable about a corrupt manager in order to correct the perversion in their thinking.

In the parable, a rich man's steward was accused of mismanaging the household finances, and was called to settle his accounts before being fired. This manager thought about his options. He wasn't strong enough to dig ditches, and he was too ashamed to beg, so he came up with a third choice. He decided to leverage his outstanding accounts in order to win friends. That way, when he was kicked out of the master's house, people would take care of him.

So this shrewd but dishonest steward went to each of the rich man's debtors, asked them how much they owed, and told them to rewrite their bills to show a reduced debt. He gave them each a huge discount. And why not? He was going to get fired anyway, so there was virtually nothing to lose if he got caught. In pure self-interest, he was trying to get himself out of a jam.

When the master found out about the steward's dealings, he commended him. He didn't commend him for his dishonesty or for his selfishness but for his ingenious methods. This manager understood how to use his momentary opportunity for long-term gain (Luke 16:1-19).

Here's how Jesus applied that lesson to His disciples: "I tell you, use worldly wealth to gain friends for yourselves, so that when it is gone, you will be welcomed into eternal dwellings" (Luke 16:9). The dishonest manager leveraged what he had in the present in order to gain a future reward. That logic and methodology is, according to Jesus, exactly how the children of light ought to think. He is telling us to use our material resources here and now with a view toward getting a future reward in eternity with God. That's how we demonstrate brilliance.

> Jesus' words make it clear: a test of our true devotion is what we do with this little thing called "money."

In explaining His parable, Jesus goes on to describe the dynamic behind this principle. "Whoever can be trusted with very little can also be trusted with much" (Luke 16:10). If we've been trustworthy in handling worldly wealth, God will trust us to handle true riches—the things of His kingdom, the things and people that matter most in life.

Do you see what Jesus is getting at? The context is money, but the promise goes a whole lot further than that. If we're faithful in small things—handling money, for example—we will be entrusted with greater things. But if we're unrighteous in small things, then we'll be unrighteous with greater things. How we handle something as mundane as money determines, to a large degree, what God blesses us with spiritually and eternally. In other words, learning to give wisely and steward our worldly wealth is basic. It's like the ABCs of faithfulness, a first step. If we don't get that down, we don't move on very far. But if we do, we step into whole new areas of blessing and opportunity. We get true riches, the kind that allows us to play a role in transforming other lives and impacting souls. We receive eternal treasures.

God is the wisest investment banker in the universe. He doesn't give us the greater riches to start off with. He gives us little tests with worldly wealth— our money—and says, "Okay, let's see where your heart is. Are you really worshiping me, or are you worshiping yourself through your stuff?" Jesus' words make it clear: a test of our true devotion is what we do with this little thing called "money."

Let's apply this to my stewardship of John Saville's money. What do you think would have happened if I gave him this report at one of our celebration meals? "John, I'm not sure how much of your money is still in the account. I'm a little bit off—I may have blown $300 or $400." I'm pretty sure John wouldn't have told me, "Chip, you're doing such a great job, I'm going to open up another checking account—this one just for you, in your name." Not a chance.

Likewise, God says to us, "If you can't be trustworthy with my temporal resources, how can you be prepared to handle responsibility in much more significant areas?" The answer should be obvious: we can't.

THE SEARCH FOR INTELLIGENT LIFE

I can't tell you the scores of conversations I've had with sincere Christians in the last 25 years as a pastor who can't understand why they're experiencing so little of God's power and see so little happen in their church or small group or ministry project. When I ask a few questions, I usually discover most Christ-followers have never connected the dots between their use of money and God's activity and blessing in their lives and significant relationships.

So I tell them that there's a better, smarter way to live … an idea so simple, it's genius. It's the generous life.

But in order for them to be faithful and trustworthy in small things like money, they need to establish their priorities. And the most basic priority in the Christian life is that God comes first. Their giving needs to reflect that.

There are two basic financial practices all of us can establish that show that God is our priority. These practices are prerequisites toward becoming generous people. The first is that faithful stewards demonstrate generosity by giving their first and best to God.

We're told in Proverbs 3:9 to honor the Lord with our wealth, the first of all our "crops." That was written to people who lived in an agriculture-based economy, but the principle clearly applies to all of us. If our priorities are right, our offerings to the Lord will come first, right off the top of our income. Not only that, our offerings will consist of the best we have. We don't want to offer God the dregs of our time, talent, or treasures. True love will offer Him the very best we have.

The Old Testament gives us several pictures of this. The harvest offering was a gift to God of the "first fruits." No one would figure out how much they had, use what they needed, and then give God what was left over. It was a gift of faith—an offering to God right up front, believing that the coming harvest would be enough to meet their needs. And the Old Testament sacrificial laws forbade people from offering animals that were sick, lame, weak, or blemished. They were to offer the best of their flocks and herds.

I recently cleaned out my garage, put everything I didn't want into plastic bags, and made a run to Goodwill. I unloaded it, got a receipt that would allow me to write it off on my taxes, and went back home. What I did in cleaning up and getting a tax write-off was wise, but it wasn't generous. I didn't want any of that stuff. Generosity is about giving from your heart, and a heartfelt gift is a high priority and of high quality.

People who work on benevolence teams for churches and ministries have told me about many of the donations they get. "People give us stuff that they would never use themselves," one of them said. "We get leftover food that no one would ever eat and worn-out clothes that no one would ever wear." It's great for people to make donations to benevolence ministries, but for most people, it isn't an act of generosity. The first sign of true generosity is that we give our first and our best, not what's left over.

The second step to generosity that reflects God as our priority is giving regularly and systematically. Generosity isn't always a matter of waiting until you're in a giving mood and then going wild with generosity. It certainly can include such moments of inspiration, but first and foremost it's a pattern.

Bright Idea
Generous givers make God and His purposes their highest priority.

Paul wrote to the church at Corinth about a collection he was taking up for the believers in Jerusalem who were going through hard financial times. He urged these Corinthians to do what the Galatian believers did: "On the first day of every week, each one of you should set aside a sum of money in keeping with his income, saving it up, so that when I come no collections will have to be made" (1 Corinthians 16:2). Paul knew that generosity is more than an occasional attitude or a feel-good response to a pressing need. It's a regular practice, and it's a spiritual habit we form that directs and protects our hearts.

Though Paul told the Corinthians to give on the first day of the week—that is, on Sunday when they gathered—he wasn't mandating weekly giving. Wages in that time were generally given weekly or even daily, so naturally that's when giving occurred. I urge people to give in the same rhythm that they receive, which is often once or twice monthly. If you get paid once a week, set aside an offering once a week. If you get paid once a month, do it once a month. If you get paid on commission, give when you receive your commission. The point isn't to fulfill a legalistic schedule; it's to give the first and the best of what you receive—regularly and systematically

This is a key concept: Generous givers make God and His purposes their highest priority. The only way to be a wise steward or manager of someone else's resources is to prioritize them. We become good, generous stewards by thinking of God first with our possessions, our time, and our talents. Just as I began asking myself what John would do in each situation as I managed his discretionary fund, we begin asking God what He would want us to do with His resources as we manage them. And the basic first steps to take are giving the first and giving the best back to God as an act of gratitude and worship.

THREE QUESTIONS SMART STEWARDS ASK

Faithful stewards are mindful of the one they represent. Not only are they good managers of their Master's money, they know who their Master is. Just as I got to know John Saville by seeing needs through his eyes, good stewards learn how to direct their Master's resources entrusted to them.

In order for us to be that kind of steward—insightful managers growing in an understanding of our Master's generosity and learning to be generous like Him—we need to regularly ask three questions:

1. Am I using the money entrusted to me in accordance with the owner's wishes?

When you look at your checking account, your bank statements, your investments, and everything else in your financial profile, do you see a clear direction toward fulfilling God's purposes and His agenda? Or do you see them fulfilling your own agenda? You'll obviously see money going toward your basic needs, as well as some going above and beyond those basic needs. God commands us to celebrate and enjoy the good things He has given. But good managers will reflect deep concern for the will of the owner and direct His resources toward His purposes.

How can we know what His purposes are? We can see some clear themes in scripture. One is the Great Commission. God is concerned about every lost person on this planet. He wants them to hear the Gospel and come to know Jesus personally. If your money is going toward reaching lost people, it's going toward His purposes.

Another of God's purposes is building up the body of Christ, the church. God wants every believer to grow to spiritual maturity and fulfill their purpose in Him. When we give toward that end, we are using His resources for His purposes.

Third, God is passionate about hurting, desperate people. He is compassionate toward those in need. If we put our money into acts of compassion and justice for those who have deep physical, emotional, and spiritual needs, our giving is aligned with His purposes. We can know we are being trustworthy in fulfilling the owner's wishes when we put His resources toward these things.

2. Am I carefully keeping an account of where the owner's funds are going?

When I met with John over lunch to celebrate the fruitfulness of our giving, I opened up his checkbook and said, "This is where your money went." This goes far beyond demonstrating that we gave a certain percentage for our "first and best" offering. Whether we're giving Him 10 percent or 50 percent, whatever's left after our offering is still His. We're just as accountable for how we spend the remaining 90 percent or the remaining 50 percent as we are for giving Him the first and best to start with.

In order to do that, we have to keep track of where the money is going. One of the clearest evidences that we are serious about being a good money manager is that we live on at least some semblance of a budget. It's impossible to be a good steward of someone else's money if we haven't determined where it will go and tracked it along the way.

The problem is that the great majority of people don't live on a budget. We pay the bills and then spend the rest somewhat randomly or without clear intentions. This is one reason personal debt is such a problem; it's easy to overspend in a credit-card culture, especially when we aren't living according to a budget.

A budget doesn't always have to be highly detailed. It's a tool for freedom and accountability, not a chain to deprive our lives of enjoyment. Mine and Theresa's is very simple—we honor the Lord with our first and best, then we pay the bills before going out and buying anything. Then we sit down and figure how much we'll need for the next two-week period for groceries, gas for the car, recreation, etc. We put the amount for each category in envelopes and live out of those envelopes. Once it's gone, it's gone; we don't go out to eat again until the next pay period. When gas money starts getting low, we adjust our plans to make it last. It's simple, but it works.

One easy and fun way to figure out how much you'll need in each area is to start tracking where your money goes. Get a little spiral notebook that you can fit in your pocket or even a note-taking or budgeting app on a mobile phone, and then every time you spend any money, even if it's just a few cents, write down the amount and what you spent it on. Do that for 30 days. Don't change your spending yet (although this exercise alone starts to make you aware of unnecessary expenditures). The point is just to find out where your money goes in a typical month.

When you're done, list categories and add up what you've spent in each category. You'll be astounded at where your money goes, and you'll see patterns and habits that will surprise you. Once you see how much you're spending in a particular area, you may decide you'd rather spend some of that on something else more worthwhile. It's a great way to start to develop a budget, to determine your priorities, and to be intentional about where your Master's money is going.

3. Am I becoming best friends with the Owner by managing His resources?

Though a lot of faithful stewardship involves sacrifice, don't let that overshadow the joy of fulfilling your Father's wishes and the celebration with Him of your fruitfulness. There's nothing legalistic in the kind of generosity we're talking about. We're becoming faithful stewards because we want to, not because we're Pharisees or martyrs, or because we want God to love us more. He'll never love us more than He loves us right now.

Generous giving and faithful stewardship create an opportunity for us to enjoy God's blessing and delight. That's part of the genius of generosity; it deepens our relationship with Him. Have a few extravagant lunches with Him to celebrate what you and He have done together with His resources. John never felt grudgingly about offering me a steak or lobster for lunch. He enjoyed the bond that developed between us as I managed his resources and reported back to him.

> Generous giving and faithful stewardship create an opportunity for us to enjoy God's blessing and delight.

When our priorities are in line, there's nothing wrong with spending money on a great vacation and enjoying the earth God made and the family He gave you. "The earth is the Lord's, and everything in it," says His Word, and He loves it when we celebrate with Him—guilt-free. Stewardship is not about depriving yourself of anything nice. It's enjoying His generosity for yourself and sharing it with others. It's living under the gaze of an infinite being who loves you and says, "First and foremost, give it and spend it in a way that's pleasing to Me and that acknowledges that I own it all. Manage it well. Then, let's celebrate. Let's rejoice. I am your Father. I love you. Every good and perfect gift comes from my hand to bless and encourage you. Let me delight over you and your faithfulness." That's what stewardship is about.

Your life will be dramatically transformed when you really realize, deep down in your heart, that everything belongs to God and He trusts you to use it well. Wake up every day asking, "Lord, what do you want me to do with this time, talent, and treasure You've given me? What would make You happiest and give me the most bang for my buck spiritually? What can I do to become a better friend with You through this process—to get to the place where we can have extravagant lunches and celebrate Your goodness, and where I can feel Your pleasure over me?" That's how a genius thinks—like a faithful, generous steward—and it will produce great joy and fruitfulness in your life.

Bright Idea
Enjoy God's generosity to you ... then share it with others.

THE GENIUS LIFE: TOM MONAGHAN

A millionaire's vow of poverty: One man's calling to give away his fortune and "die broke"

Tom Monaghan was outwardly as successful as a businessman could be. The innovative founder of Domino's Pizza grew up in poverty, but at the peak of his personal empire, he owned the largest pizza delivery chain in the world, the Detroit Tigers baseball team, and plenty of expensive cars and collectibles. At one point, 54 percent of all the pizzas delivered in the U.S. were delivered by his stores. He was at the top of his industry.

But reading C.S. Lewis' *Mere Christianity* one night, Monaghan came across a passage about pride that hit him right between the eyes. He saw himself in Lewis' words and was suddenly aware that all of his hard work

"My main goal is to help as many people as possible to get to heaven," Tom says. "And I want my money to go where it does the most good and saves the most souls."

was based not only on having more, but on having more than others. "I was too obsessed with impressing people," he says. Sobered by the realization that he was the proudest person he knew—and that pride was the basis for all other sins—he decided to rededicate his life to God.

Monaghan decided to give up all his "toys" and took what he calls a "millionaire's vow of poverty." He eventually sold

Domino's Pizza and determined to devote the rest of his life to giving away what he had in order to help people know Christ. He knows he can't take his money with him, and he doesn't want to just leave it to others to decide how it is given away. He has taken care of the needs of his family, but the rest is being leveraged for eternity. He wants to die broke and has put himself in a position to do exactly that.

"My main goal is to help as many people as possible get to Heaven," Monaghan says. "And I want my money to go where it does the most good and saves the most souls." He has founded a Catholic university (Ave Maria University in Florida) where he has pledged the majority of his remaining resources in addition to working full time to raise money for its mission in an effort to help build God's kingdom

Monaghan's sense of satisfaction and fulfillment is profound. "My life is so right for the way God made me," he says. "I believe I am doing exactly what God wants me to do. And I feel so privileged that He gave me the wisdom to see it."

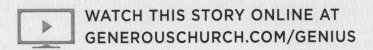 **WATCH THIS STORY ONLINE AT GENEROUSCHURCH.COM/GENIUS**

Chapter 2
DISCUSSION & REFLECTION

The following is a summary of the ideas and questions from Chapter 2. Use them for personal reflection or small group discussion, and consider journaling to record your thoughts and impressions.

BRIGHT IDEAS

Which of these "Bright Ideas" has the most meaning for you? Why?

- Stewardship is the path. Generosity is the adventure.

- Generous givers make God and His purposes their highest priority.

- Enjoy God's generosity to you ... then share it with others.

IMPACT FROM TOM MONAGHAN'S STORY

Why do you think Tom Monaghan wasn't satisfied with his success? In what ways was his wealth based on pride?

Have you discovered any underlying motives in your pursuits for material things? If so, what?

Why do you think Tom Monaghan now feels more fulfillment in giving things away than he did in accumulating them?

REFLECTION QUESTIONS

1 What has God deposited into your life and asked you to steward? Make a list?

2 How could seeing stewardship as a privilege and opportunity change your view of giving and generosity?

3 Good stewards are good managers. Where do you need to do a better job of managing the resources that God has entrusted to you?

4 Chip said "faithful stewards demonstrate generosity by giving their first and best to God." Practically speaking, what does it look like for you and your family to give your first and best to God?

5 Chip mentions three ways to give to God's purposes. Which one of these do you need to be more generous toward?

- The Great Commission (spreading the Gospel)
- The Church
- Hurting people

Chapter 3

WHY GOD PROSPERS GENEROUS PEOPLE

A man was once lost in the desert and close to dying of thirst. He had wandered aimlessly through the hot sand for days, growing weaker by the moment. If he didn't find help soon, his life would be over. Finally, he saw some palm trees in the distance—an oasis, he assumed. He stumbled forward, hoping to have enough strength to make it.

When he arrived at the trees, he noticed something strange about this oasis. There was no pool of water, no bubbling spring. Instead, he saw only a pump. And beside the pump were two objects: a small jar of water and a note on a piece of parchment.

He picked up the note and read it. It explained how the leather gasket within the pump must be saturated with water in order for the pump to function. There was just enough water in the jar. The note warned the reader not to drink from the jar. Every drop needed to be poured into the opening at the base of the pump in order to soak the dry gasket. As the leather softened and expanded, an unlimited supply of water would then be available. The note concluded with instructions to refill the container for the next traveler.

The man faced a high-stakes choice. He was dying of thirst. Would he drink the only water visibly available? Or would he believe the note and pour out the only water in sight in order to prime the pump? If he drank the water in the jar, it would save him—at least for a time. But would it be enough to keep him going until he found another source of water? Probably not. On the other hand, if he believed the note and the dry, old pump didn't work, he would have squandered his only chance at survival. It seemed foolish to pour his only available water into a hole. But doing so could lead to an unlimited supply.

That parable—made popular in an old song by the Kingston Trio called "Desert Pete"—is a great picture of the faith required in order to be generous. Great promises are given to generous people, but we can only receive those promises by first giving away our treasures. It doesn't seem very wise to give what you can see in exchange for what you can't see. In fact, it feels risky. It requires faith.

That's where many of us find ourselves when we decide to become generous, faithful stewards. We start with the basics—giving the first and best of what we have, and giving systematically and regularly—but that's just the beginning of the journey. The degree of faith required of us only increases from there. That's why the average Christian only gives about 2.5 percent of his or her income to the work of God's kingdom. Giving feels risky.

Yet we've seen how generosity is a win-win proposition. It's one of the smartest approaches to life a person can have. God makes extravagant promises for those who step out and give generously, and those promises are certain. Those who don't believe that miss out on a blessing, but those who do believe it will act on their belief and reap unimaginable rewards. They may not see those rewards in the here and now—although very often they will—but they will see them. Their investment will pay off spiritually, relationally, eternally, and quite often financially. God honors faith (Hebrews 11:6).

GIVING OF LOGICAL PROPORTIONS

Faith is the key to becoming habitually generous and experiencing the joy of giving. And our faith gets stretched when we understand the principle of giving proportionally. Generous people give proportionally to the way God has blessed them.

Bright Idea
Faith increases giving, and giving increases faith.

It was a monumental breakthrough for me when I started thinking in terms of percentages rather than amounts. When I was a kid, my mom would give me a quarter to put in the offering plate. Later that grew to a dollar out of my allowance, or even $5 every once in a while. When I later became a Christian, I would sometimes put $20 in the offering plate—and assume the angels were marveling over my generosity. It wasn't bad to give $20—that was my frame of reference then, and at least I was growing—but when I stepped back and compared that to my total income, I realized that wasn't very generous at all.

Earlier, we looked at Paul's instructions to the Corinthians about setting aside their offerings regularly. In that same verse, Paul introduced the principle of proportionality: "On the first day of every week, each one of you should set aside a sum of money in keeping with his income" (1 Corinthians 16:2, italics added). That simply means that those who make a lot of money should give more than those who make a little money. As our income grows, so should our giving.

This trips a lot of young Christians up, but it's a blind spot even for some who have been believers for a long time. Years ago, the church where I was pastor was interviewing a man for a significant position of leadership. This man was a godly guy—he knew God's Word and taught it well, he had a great reputation, and all of us thought he was a great pick for the position. One of the steps we always went through before putting people in an important leadership role was to have our financial officer look at their stewardship report. That may seem a little arbitrary to some people, but we did this for two reasons: (1) we believed leaders should model Christlike character and should exemplify the lifestyle we were calling the rest of the church to emulate; and (2) a person's record of giving can be a very accurate measure of his or her spiritual maturity and priorities because of the close connection between one's heart and treasure. As the pastor, I never knew the numbers for anyone's giving, but did want to know if those being considered for leadership were giving biblically.

The candidate for the position had a great job with a high income, and he gave to the church regularly. But we noticed that his level of giving was disproportionately low. Were there some factors we didn't know about? Was he generously giving to kingdom work through other avenues? Were there family members in need or circumstances that would explain the apparent contradiction? We weren't sure. So an elder and I arranged to meet with him and open up this sensitive and personal conversation about his stewardship. We told him

> God wants us to step out in faith and increase our giving as He increases our income.

we thought he was the right man for the job, but there was one matter we were concerned about. And we just put the issue out on the table.

I'll never forget his answer. "Oh, you know what? I can explain that," he said. He went on to tell us how his job had taken him out of town a lot that year because of a project he was working on. He had missed church more than usual, so his giving was low for the year.

I knew this man was godly and teachable. He had a humble spirit. This was just one of his blind spots. He had somehow gotten it in his mind that his generosity toward God's work applied when he was at church but not when he was on the road. As a result, not only was he giving very irregularly; he was giving only a small fraction of his income.

God invites us to share His joy in giving extravagantly. He wants us to step out in faith and increase our giving as He increases our income.

GOD, THE BLESSER

When we talk about giving proportionally—i.e., by percentage rather than amount—try not to think in terms of the traditional 10 percent tithe. That's a proportional gift, but it's not always the best reflection of our ability to give or our desire to do so. Our capacity and passion for generosity should never be limited by a standard figure. It's much better to drop our assumptions and expectations and ask God to lead us to the proportion that best reflects our heart and our income.

There has been much written and debated about giving a tithe (10 percent) as the first portion of our income to God. The tithe was instituted before the law of Moses. The Israelites actually paid multiple tithes a year under their theocracy—their giving amounted to about 23 percent of their total income. Jesus would instruct the Pharisees of His day to realign their hearts and recognize the worship that God wants is love, mercy, and justice without neglecting the required 10 percent under the law.

Unfortunately, this whole discussion usually misses the spirit and purpose of the genius of generosity. Questions—like, "Do you pay the tithe on the gross or the net?"—quickly emerge. The real question behind these questions seems to be, "How little can I give and still fulfill what's required of me?" That isn't generosity, that's simply an obligation.

My counsel is to encourage people to start with a tithe as an excellent beginning in their generosity journey as a reminder that as God blesses and expands their income, we have the privilege of proportionally laying up more treasure for ourselves and experiencing the joy and thrill of meeting needs that change people's lives. And instead of giving exactly 10 percent, consider giving 9 or 11 percent, just to prevent a legalistic, rigid mindset that is permanently locked onto one standard amount.

> Unless God begins to move in my heart—and my wallet, my schedule, and my to-do list— I'll never receive His best for me.

The key principle here is that this isn't about money in itself; it's about learning to live under God's lordship and experiencing His blessing. Unless God begins to move in my heart—and my wallet, my schedule, and my to-do list—I'll never receive His best for me.

God blesses generous people. The greatest blessings are to live under His authority, experience His power and peace, develop deep relationships with Him and others, know His purposes, and watch Him begin to use our lives and change the lives of others. The material blessing is pretty far down on the list of what we receive from God when we're generous. He has plenty of resources; He isn't desperately waiting for us to give ours. His desire is not to get our money but to get our hearts and bless our lives.

We see this dynamic clearly in Paul's words about sowing and reaping: "Whoever sows sparingly will also reap sparingly, and whoever sows generously will also reap generously" (2 Corinthians 9:6). We don't have to worry about God letting us down because we're being too generous. The same passage tells us that He is able to make all grace abound to us so that we'll have all we need in every situation (2 Corinthians 9:8). He promises abundance for every good work.

WHY DOES GOD PROSPER US?

God blesses us because He's a good God. He loves us and wants to see us prosper. But there's a reason He blesses us with abundance. He has an agenda: to bless us so we can bless others.

This is where a lot of people get hung up, and the result is something we call the "prosperity gospel." In other words, many people see God's blessing in response to our generosity as an end in itself. It becomes a "give in order to get" proposition, and that completely violates the spirit or the heart behind what Scripture teaches. God does not prosper us simply so we can get a larger house, a faster car, or a more impressive wardrobe. That's not the point. He blesses us to put us in a position to be conduits of His grace and goodness to others.

The prosperity gospel turns wealth into an end in itself. You give a certain amount, then in response to your faith, God multiplies your gift and gives it back to you. Why? So you can have more to spend on yourself. But that's not what Scripture teaches, and that's not God's purpose. God always blesses those who are generous, but it isn't always a material blessing. His gifts are often much more profound than that. And when He does bless us materially, He does it so we can use more of His resources for kingdom purposes. If we don't, we squander a great opportunity to bear eternal fruit.

This is the principle behind Jesus' familiar parable of the talents. Those who did something with what they received were given more. The one who protected what he had learned that even what he had would be taken away. When we are generous, God often gives us more so we can give more. I love the way Randy Alcorn puts it in his book *The Treasure Principle*: "God prospers me not to raise my standard of living but to raise my standard of giving." In my own life, as I was faithful with John Saville's money, he would replenish the account so I could give even more of his resources away. Likewise, God blesses generous people with increased resources for a purpose.

RICH IN EVERY WAY

Let's take another look at that passage in 2 Corinthians, where Paul wrote about sowing and reaping. It describes God's ability to make His grace "abound"—to overflow in our lives. But then Paul uses an agricultural metaphor to explain why:

> As it is written: "He has scattered abroad his gifts to the poor; his righteousness endures forever." Now he who supplies seed to the sower and bread for food will also supply and increase your store of seed and will enlarge the harvest of your righteousness. You will be made rich in every way so that you can be generous on every occasion, and through us your generosity will result in thanksgiving to God (2 Corinthians 9:9-11).

God gives seed to the sower—that's the farmer's resource. To put the agricultural metaphor in spiritual terms, that's all the money God ever gives us. The farmer takes part of what he receives and makes bread with it. He has to take care of himself and his family. But there's also a "store of seed," and he has to decide what to do with it. Does he keep building bigger barns to hold all his seed? Or does he reinvest the seed in the ground so it will multiply? Paul writes about an increase in the store of seed so that the harvest will increase. And in the context of generosity, this increase is a "harvest of righteousness."

Do you see the principle? God wants to bless our lives spiritually, relationally, and materially—or, as Paul says, "in every way." Why? So we can be generous "on every occasion." He pours out His blessing on us so our own needs can be met, but also so we can reinvest in others. This is how the storehouse multiplies and our "harvest of righteousness" increases. Every step of generosity, each one a step of faith, is met with greater reward. The result is thanksgiving to God.

That's God's genius in generosity. He guards our hearts against greed by blessing us when we give away what we have. In doing so, we have to keep our focus on Him and depend on Him. Then He does something amazing: He transforms us and lives around us through our generosity. We are blessed in order to bless others, and the cycle of generosity begins again.

Blessing others doesn't mean we can't enjoy His blessings ourselves. If your priorities are right and God gives you a nice car, a nice home, and nice possessions, thank Him. If He allows you to eat well every night, praise Him for His generosity. Austerity isn't the goal. The point is that if He increases our income, He has a bigger agenda than padding our bank account or raising our standard of living. We get more seed (money) so we can sow it into the needs of others so we can reap a greater harvest.

Bright Idea
Those blessed by God become blessers for God.

So let me ask you: If your standard of living and income has increased over the years, has your generosity increased proportionally? Is giving a duty to fulfill or an adventure of transforming the lives of those around you as you invest God's money according to His wishes?

BEATING GENEROSITY'S BIGGEST COMPETITOR

I firmly believe that the perception that stewardship and giving are guilt-laden responsibilities is depriving most Christians of one of the greatest joys of life. If I could sum up what the Bible teaches about giving in one statement, it would be this: Generous living produces emotional happiness. Remember the picture of Scrooge—the tightwad who was miserable while he was pinching pennies but exuberantly joyful when he learned to give? That's a Biblical picture.

But there's a major competitor to this joyful life: greed. And I know two ways to prevent it:

1. Refuse to chase the wind.

That's how Solomon, the source of so much wisdom in Scripture, expressed it. Toward the end of his life—after accumulating all of his wealth, building his buildings, and marrying hundreds of wives—he wrote about the futility of it all. He had done it all; Scripture says he tasted all of life and withheld nothing from himself. And after all of that, he penned Ecclesiastes, a book about his life experiences. So what did he say about wealth?

> *"When I surveyed all that my hands had done and what I had toiled to achieve, everything was meaningless, a chasing after the wind; nothing was gained under the sun" (Ecclesiastes 2:11).*

Theresa and I were walking around a downtown city once and came across a little book called *The Rich Are Different*. It's full of quotations and anecdotes about the wealthy. One of the stories in it is about Osman Ali, the Nizam of Hyderabad, a potentate considered to be the richest man in the world in the 1940s. When he died, his rooms were found to be full of stacks of currency eaten by rats and gems in color-coded safes: red for rubies, green for emeralds, blue for sapphires. That's a great picture of what Solomon describes when he says that whoever loves money never has enough (Ecclesiastes 5:10).

Numerous wealthy people agree. John D. Rockefeller said, "I have made many millions, but they have brought me no happiness." Andrew Carnegie said, "Millionaires rarely smile." John Jacob Astor, one of the wealthiest men in the world, said he was the most miserable man in the world. Wealth is a high-maintenance endeavor, and it's draining. It's exactly what Solomon warned about: "The sleep of a laborer is sweet, whether he eats little or much, but the abundance of a rich man permits him no sleep" (Ecclesiastes 5:12). The more you have, the more you have to maintain—and the more you realize the real limitations of wealth in bringing real satisfaction and joy to your life. Wise people eventually see the folly in chasing the wind.

Bright Idea
Generous living is joyful living.

One of the clearest examples of the misery of hoarding wealth is the case of Hetty Green. She inherited several million dollars and multiplied it many times through the stock market. Still, she lived in flophouses, resold used newspapers and empty bottles, and carried crackers in her purse to avoid the expense of restaurants. Her son broke his leg in an accident, and even though her annual income exceeded $7 million, she tried to have him treated at a charity ward. When she was recognized and turned away because she wasn't a charity case, she got angry and determined to heal his wounds herself. Eventually, his leg had to be amputated.

In Hetty Green's case, hoarding wealth was sick. In all cases, it's futile. In itself, it never brings happiness, and it can be lost at any time. Green was an extreme example, for sure, but her example makes the point powerfully. The real question is: How are you and I doing the same thing in far more subtle ways? As Solomon said, chasing after wealth is like chasing after the wind.

As we've said, wealth is not wrong. The Bible never forbids having a lot of money. Abraham had a lot; so did David. Both were blessed greatly and used mightily by God. Many key figures in the New Testament church were landowners, but they used their wealth to finance the ministry of Jesus and the early church. The Bible doesn't condemn wealth; it condemns pursuing wealth and seeking fulfillment in it. Refuse to chase after the wind.

2. Refuse to view generosity as depriving yourself of something good.

Most of us have been brainwashed into believing what I call "the small-pie syndrome." This mentality says that there's only so much to go around, and if I give away what I have, I'm going to lose it. The idea is that if I give my piece of the pie away, I'll never get it back again.

The flaw in that thinking is that the kingdom of God is full of big pies that multiply. If I give away my piece of the pie, God will probably give me two more. Then I can give those two away and probably get four more. Obviously, that isn't a formula. But God doesn't have a small-pie mentality. We can't ever out-give Him.

Look at what Paul instructed Timothy:

> Command those who are rich in this present world not to be arrogant nor to put their hope in wealth, which is so uncertain, but to put their hope in God, who richly provides us with everything for our enjoyment. Command them to do good, to be rich in good deeds, and to be generous and willing to share. In this way they will lay up treasure for themselves as a firm foundation for the coming age, so that they may take hold of the life that is truly life (1 Timothy 6:17-19).

You'll see a warning in that passage against chasing after the wind, just as Solomon described. Wealth is "uncertain," to say the least. But notice where we are to put our hope: "in God." Why? Because He "richly provides us with everything for our enjoyment." There's no small-pie mentality in that instruction. Sure, if you give away some money and possessions, you'll miss out on something temporal every once in a while. But you'll also gain a lot, both now and in eternity—"a firm foundation for the coming age," to be specific. In the big picture, generosity is not deprivation. It's a shrewd investment for today and tomorrow.

HOW TO EXPERIENCE THE PROMISE

God wants to bless your life spiritually, relationally, and materially. Why? Because He loves you, of course; that's part of His nature and His desire for you. But He has more in mind than simply blessing you for your own enjoyment. He does it also so you can bless others.

The key to this dynamic is faith. In order to give away your resources, you have to believe God is your provider—and that He's good and wants to bless you. The Bible is clear that God honors generosity with promises of great blessing, but in order to experience this blessing, you have to believe what God says and act on it. Like the wanderer in the desert who had to pour out his only available water to get an abundant supply, we have to pour out what we have in order to experience God's abundant provision. The more we demonstrate that kind of trust in Him, the more He entrusts to us.

What would it look like in your life right now to pour out some of the "water" in that "jar"—to experience some risk, have some faith, and love someone else? It may not seem very safe, but it's one of the smartest moves you can make. Go ahead—give it a try.

THE GENIUS LIFE: DREW M.

A young giver's journey of generosity

Drew's first attempt at raising money wasn't very successful. At 13, he and three friends—Brandon, Phil, and Kyle—wanted to build another level to a tree fort at the conference center where they were staying. So they solicited sponsors to give a dollar per hour for a sit-in . . . and raised less than $60 from family and friends. The fort expansion didn't look very promising.

But one night at the conference center, a missionary from India spoke on how to sponsor children for a dollar a day. It was the first time the boys had heard how they could personally be involved in missions, and they got an idea. They would organize another sit-in, this time for a bigger cause. They found enough sponsors to raise $7,500, a grandfather's matching pledge raised it to $15,000, and another donor's matching pledge doubled it to $30,000. And four young men learned a lifelong lesson in the power of generosity.

> "God brings up different [giving] opportunities," Drew says, and the ones that appeal to him are usually those that involve more than a financial gift. "It's cool to give where you're also investing your time, your thoughts, and your prayers."

Drew, now a senior at Wheaton College, credits his parents with instilling kingdom values into him and demonstrating a generous lifestyle, and he has continued to give over the years. The causes he supports are as varied as his interests—a country he has studied at school, or a ministry whose impact he has seen. "God brings up different opportunities," he says, and the ones that appeal to him are usually those that involve more than a financial gift. "It's cool to give where you're also investing your time, your thoughts, and your prayers."

Since the experience at the conference center, Drew has developed a broader perspective on giving, mainly through giving experiences that didn't go well. When he and his friends raised money to sponsor Indian children, they had nothing to gain from it personally. "But sometimes you're expecting a really good story or great results—like you can leverage God through your good deeds, and then He's compelled to bless you."

So Drew tries to take himself completely out of the equation— to give because he wants to, not because he's expecting something back. Like most generous givers, he has had to overcome the assumption that "giving X amount of dollars will produce X amount of happiness." He finds giving to be more fulfilling when "the primary craving is more about Christ Himself than His blessings."

 WATCH THIS STORY ONLINE AT GENEROUSCHURCH.COM/GENIUS

Chapter 3
DISCUSSION & REFLECTION

The following is a summary of the ideas and questions from Chapter 3. Use them for personal reflection or small group discussion, and consider journaling to record your thoughts and impressions.

BRIGHT IDEAS

Which of these "Bright Ideas" has the most meaning for you? Why?

- Faith increases giving, and giving increases faith.

- Those blessed by God become blessers for God.

- Generous living is joyful living.

IMPACT FROM DREW'S STORY

Do you think it's important to take yourself "out of the equation" when you give? If so, why?

How can knowing the blessings for generosity shape our motives for giving? What can we do to keep our motives pure?

Why is it important to demonstrate a generous lifestyle for the younger generation?

REFLECTION QUESTIONS

1 Randy Alcorn says "God prospers me not to raise my standard of living but to raise my standard of giving." How do you respond to his statement? What are the personal implications of his statement?

2 How would you need to simplify your life in order to be more generous?

3 Solomon said chasing after wealth is like chasing after the wind. Do some self-assessment. How much time and energy is devoted to chasing after money and stuff?

4 Read 1 Timothy 6:17-19 slowly and carefully (see end of chapter). What phrase or sentence most speaks to what you need to hear right now?

5 God blesses us with abundance so that we can bless others. Who is it this week that you need to bless with your generosity?

Chapter 4

HOW GOD MEASURES GENEROSITY

I n the time of Jesus, there was a receptacle outside the temple. It was a place where people would come and drop off various monetary offerings—financial gifts for temple upkeep and the worship that was practiced at this holy site. This spot became somewhat of a stage for some of the religious leaders; a few of them would even blow a trumpet when they were going to put money in it so everyone could see their generous gift. Their motives were a little off, to say the least.

One day, Jesus and His disciples were sitting near this temple treasury and Jesus noticed a widow walk up to the box and drop two small coins into it. Few people would have noticed this seemingly ordinary event, but Jesus did. In fact, He pointed it out to His disciples. It became the occasion for an object lesson. "'I tell you the truth,' he said, 'this poor widow has put in more than all the others. All these people gave their gifts out of their wealth; but she out of her poverty put in all she had to live on.'" Jesus commended her gift because she gave "more" than anyone else (Luke 21:1-4).

Unfortunately, a lot of people misapply this familiar story. The main point, they believe, is that it doesn't matter how much someone gives. It's really just a matter of the heart. If your heart is right, any amount—even a few pennies—is a pleasing offering to God. Though true, that isn't the primary purpose of this passage.

Bright Idea
God measures generosity not by the size of the gift but by the size of the sacrifice.

Clearly, Jesus wasn't talking about amounts, either large or small. Rather, her example points to another principle: God measures generosity by the level of sacrifice it involves. This widow gave "more than all the others" because her gift put her at risk. It was all she had to live on. In her gift, she demonstrated more wisdom than all the "experts" at the temple. She gave out of a generous heart that put her own needs behind her desire to honor God.

That isn't how we normally measure gifts. We see large donations and call the giver "generous" because of the size of the gift. God measures generosity not by the size of the gift but by the size of the sacrifice. How do you know when you've given sacrificially? The litmus test is this: You've given sacrificially when your giving impacts your lifestyle.

FOR THE LOVE OF GOD

Generosity is progressive. It begins with the basics—giving the first and best, and giving regularly and systematically. Then it proceeds to an understanding of proportionality—giving according to the level at which God has blessed you materially. But even more significant is the heart behind the gift.

You see, true generosity is formed from a special intertwining of sacrifice and thoughtful, voluntary worship. That's another reason generosity is so genius. It's all about our love for God. It's a spiritual act of worship. It's progressive, reaching deeper and deeper into our lives and reflecting a deepening and joyful relationship with our Heavenly Father.

This loving generosity was on grand display in the New Testament. Paul wrote quite a bit about how generous certain churches were—not to impress anyone but to spur others on to greater devotion. In 2 Corinthians 8-9, a passage we've touched on briefly, he showcased the sacrificial giving of the Macedonian churches.

> *Out of the most severe trial, their overflowing joy and their extreme poverty welled up in rich generosity. For I testify that they gave as much as they were able, and even beyond their ability. Entirely on their own, they urgently pleaded with us for the privilege of sharing in this service to the saints (2 Corinthians 8:2-4).*

Life was hard for these churches in Macedonia. They were in "extreme poverty." But they heard about their Jewish brothers who were suffering from a famine, and they wanted to give. No one coerced them or made them feel guilty. They voluntarily made sacrifices, and they considered it a privilege. These believers who didn't have much gave to other believers who had even less. It cost them something; they put themselves at risk. That's a great picture of real generosity and sacrifice.

You can only give that way if you see "your" possessions as God's and hold them loosely. That's why, in one sense, my pact with John Saville was such a perfect picture of our stewardship of God's resources. But in another sense, it wasn't really a sacrifice for me to give away his money. It wasn't mine, and I wasn't attached to it. Our handling of our bank accounts is another story. We've developed a sense of responsibility (and even attachment) to our personal finances. We're used to reaping the consequences, both good and bad, of our decisions. When we choose to make an offering to the Lord, we're choosing not to spend our money on something else. It feels like a sacrifice, and it should.

A story in the Old Testament gives us another vivid picture of the heart of sacrifice. David had ordered a count of his military, contrary to God's will, and the result was a plague on his country. The Lord told David through the words of a prophet to go offer a burnt offering on the threshing floor of a local resident named Araunah. So David went and explained to Araunah the Lord's command to build an altar and stop the plague with a sacrifice to God.

When Araunah heard David's request, he offered not only the land but also the oxen and materials for the sacrifice as a gift. But David insisted on paying. Why? "I will not sacrifice to the Lord my God burnt offerings that cost me nothing" (2 Samuel 24:24). David understood a critical truth: sacrifice is a necessary part of giving an offering.

We can give in a way that doesn't affect us at all—our lifestyle isn't impacted, our plans aren't affected, and we still buy everything we were going to buy anyway. That still counts as giving—and can still be considered "generous"—but it isn't sacrificial. It pales in comparison to the way some people give. I've seen a mom and two small kids sacrifice getting new toys and new clothes for Christmas so they could meet the needs of others in our church. I've seen a church leader delay remodeling his house for two years so he could give to a project that would serve the rest of the body. I've seen people cancel their cable service, stop eating out, or postpone a vacation in order to meet an immediate need in the Lord's work. Those are little sacrifices compared to the widow in Jesus'

> When we give generously, it eventually needs to cost us something.

story, but they capture a giving heart that most pleases our heavenly Father (Hebrews 13:16).

When we give generously, it eventually needs to cost us something. But sacrifice shouldn't arise solely from a knee-jerk reaction to a big need or a response to pressure. On the contrary, it's a lifestyle. It flows out of a heart of worship. It's an interaction between you and God, something as biblical as praying or reading your Bible, and like those disciplines, genuine generosity requires a level of intentionality.

Bright Idea
Generosity isn't an act. It's a way of life.

Let's go back to 2 Corinthians 9. In this collection Paul is taking up for the famine relief effort in Jerusalem, he tells the Corinthians to make sure their good intentions translate into follow-through. He wants them to be thoughtful about it, to plan ahead. Then after that landmark verse about those who sow generously will reap generously, he tells them that real generosity is voluntary and joyful. "Each man should give what he has decided in his heart to give, not reluctantly or under compulsion, for God loves a cheerful giver" (2 Corinthians 9:7). It's an act of worship.

I know people who apply this verse by saying that they won't give unless they feel joyful about it. That misses the point. If I waited to read my Bible until I was enthusiastic, I'd read it about half as often as I do. If I only showed Theresa my love when I felt particularly loving, she wouldn't get all the love she deserves. If I prayed only when I felt joyful, it wouldn't happen nearly as often as it should. That's human nature; our feelings shouldn't dictate what we do out of obedience and love. The point is that the kind of giving that most excites our heavenly Father is the kind that flows out of a willingness to express devotion to God. It comes from a heart of worship that isn't under compulsion but has a desire to please Him. In fact, when it comes to generosity, God makes it clear that money is an important beginning step but far from what the genius of generosity is all about.

MONEY IS ONLY THE BEGINNING

God invites us to enter into deeper levels of generosity. He wants to give us far more than most of us are ready or willing to receive. The following three truths will help us become the kind of generous people we want to be.

1. Generosity always begins with God.

Generosity is the visible expression of His infinite, incomprehensible love for us. We can be generous because we've seen the overflow of His heart toward us. James 1:17 tells us that every good thing, every perfect gift comes from the Father of light in whom there is no variation or shifting shadow. Every good thing we have, even down to the air we breathe, is a gift from Him because He loves us.

Paul wrote extravagant words about God's love for us:

> *I kneel before the Father, from whom his whole family in heaven and on earth derives its name. I pray that out of his glorious riches he may strengthen you with power through his Spirit in your inner being, so that Christ may dwell in your hearts through faith. And I pray that you, being rooted and established in love, may have power, together with all the saints, to grasp how wide and long and high and deep is the love of Christ, and to know this love that surpasses knowledge—that you may be filled to the measure of all the fullness of God (Ephesians 3:14-19).*

When we begin to grasp this—that we are the objects of God's infinite, unconditional, incomprehensible love—we experience a profound change in perspective and personal identity. This book is not really about money;

that's just a symptom. This is about understanding God's extravagant love. He loves you not because you've done something right, nor because you understand Him well, not because you've earned His favor, but because He just does. It's who He is. And when we begin to grasp His love and generosity toward us, we begin to become generous ourselves. We live securely inside His kingdom. He knows our needs and wants to bless us. That rubs off on us. We want to bless others as well.

I would challenge you to pray slowly through this passage in Ephesians for the next 30 days. Let it sink down into the depths of your heart. Once it does, that kind of extravagant love will begin to take root in you, and you will begin to express it back to God and toward others.

2. Our generosity is the visible expression of our love for God.

On the last night of His ministry on earth with His disciples, Jesus told His followers that whoever had His commandments and kept them were the ones who loved Him. In other words, knowing the right thing to do and doing it is a litmus test of whether you love Him. We live in a time in which a lot of Christians think loving Him is about singing a song and having a positive emotional feeling about God, sporadically doing good deeds for someone, or participating in a worthy cause. Although these can be positive experiences in our spiritual journey, the truth is this: Knowing what He says and doing it are the real evidence of our love.

That means loving Him isn't about how we feel at the moment. In fact, we are probably loving Him most when we least feel like doing what's right and do it anyway, just because He said so. Parents understand this; when you're in the middle of watching a favorite show or a great ballgame and one of the kids asks for your help, you probably aren't initially excited to get up and deal with it. But what's the loving response? You act on what's best for your kids. That's love.

When you wake up in the morning and don't feel like reading your Bible but choose to meet with God anyway, that's a choice that reflects love.

When you pray even when you don't feel like it, that may take more love than praying when your spiritual passion is strong and motivation is high. This plays out in our lives in numerous ways all the time. And it's easy to see how this applies to our generosity. Genuine generosity is how we express our love for God, whether or not that expression matches our feelings at the moment.

3. Generous living begins with money and possessions, but it applies to every area of our lives.

Our material possessions are just the start. Our sacrifice and worship get really serious when we start to offer our time, reputation, future, dreams, and everything else we cling to. Romans 12:1 tells us that our spiritual act of worship is to offer our bodies—even our entire selves— to God as a living sacrifice. We lay ourselves down at the altar and say, "Here I am, Lord." I am most generous with God when I tell Him "all I am" and "all I have" is His to use as he sees fit. That includes finances, but it involves so much more. Generous giving involves every area of life, not just possessions.

Bright Idea
True generosity doesn't stop with possessions. It starts with them.

Many people are gripped with fear when they think of becoming a "living sacrifice." What if they end up working on another continent under extreme hardship for the sake of the Gospel? What if God takes away their job or their standard of living? What if he tells them never to get married? While those things are certainly possible, those fears grow out of a warped view of God. God is not a harsh killjoy; He is a kind and benevolent Father who always has our highest and best interests in mind. If and when sacrifice is called for, it is always linked to God's intention to give us far better than we could ever imagine (Ephesians 3:20). He usually works through your desires and convictions, not against them, to accomplish His purpose for our lives. The bigger issue is whether you're living with a heart of sacrifice and a desire to worship Him—or, to put it another way, whether your sense of gratitude causes you to want to hold nothing back from Him. Real love and worship are accompanied by a desire to give.

Let me challenge you to try an exercise. Take a sheet of paper and list every blessing you can think of from the last year. Have fun with it; write down everything that comes to mind. Use more than one sheet, if necessary. When you get down to "the air I breathe," you're probably near the end. Then look at that sheet and think about all that the God of the universe has done for you. Let the natural response to those gifts begin to flow from your heart. Let that awareness draw you to experience God like you never have before.

GOD'S GRADUATE SCHOOL OF GENEROSITY: THE INCARNATION

God could have chosen a number of ways to enter into this planet, but the way He did it is brilliant. It reflects true generosity—in Himself and in the people He chose to use for His story. If we look at the Christmas story through the lens of generosity, I believe you'll see that our possessions are only the training wheels of His graduate school in generosity as people respond to Him.

Let's start with the magi. These "wise men," as we know them, saw some things in the stars and realized that someone special was about to be born. They traveled to see Him, bringing some of their treasures with them to give Him. Think about that; they didn't know much about Judaism or the Jewish Messiah, but they saw in the heavens a revelation of a new king. Somehow they knew they were to follow a particular star pointing them to the birthplace of this king. And in their limited knowledge, they brought valuable gifts of gold, incense, and myrrh.

When they finally got to Jerusalem, they asked for help. After all, they only had some basic information, a rough picture of what would happen. So the experts they asked—the Jewish scribes and religious leaders—told them that a Messiah had been foretold by their prophets. They pointed the magi to Bethlehem, and, after a visit with a king with another agenda, took their gifts to the coming King. They didn't know much, but they knew the basics: you give a king the best of what you have.

Another group of people in this story gave their time to the new King. The shepherds were on the hills outside of Jerusalem just doing their job. In terms of social status, they were probably lowest people around. Suddenly, they were surrounded by angels announcing the birth of the Messiah. When the angels left, how did they respond? They left their sheep and went into the town to see the baby. And after they saw Him, they spread the word about what they had seen.

The shepherds didn't give their money to the King; they gave their time. Unlike the magi, they had a clear revelation of what was happening. The angels spelled it out for them. And they responded by stopping their work, going into town to see this new child, and then telling everyone they met about what they had witnessed. They had the privilege of becoming the first evangelists because they responded to God in obedience and genuine devotion.

Let's look next at Joseph. God didn't ask for his money or his time—he would give a lot of both to his newborn son over the next few years. That came with the responsibilities of fatherhood. No, God asked Joseph to sacrifice his reputation.

Joseph and Mary were betrothed to each other. Their families had agreed on the marriage, and the future bride and groom were spending time apart in preparation for the wedding. The couple was certainly excited about their future together, and Joseph genuinely loved and cared for his bride. When he found out she was pregnant, it must have rocked his world.

THE INCARNATION:
A GRADUATE COURSE IN GENEROSITY

YOUR MOST PRECIOUS POSSESSION — THE FATHER John 3:16

YOUR LIFE — JESUS Mark 10:45

YOUR FUTURE — MARY Luke 1:26-38

YOUR REPUTATION — JOSEPH Matthew 1:18-24

YOUR TIME — THE SHEPHERDS Luke 2:15-17

YOUR MONEY — THE MAGI Matthew 2:11

THE GENEROSITY STAIRCASE

When we look back on this story, we see centuries of prophecy being beautifully fulfilled in a miraculous birth. Joseph didn't. All he knew was that his fiancée was pregnant and that he wasn't the father. In Jewish custom, a betrothal could only be broken by divorce—or the death of the bride or groom, which was a real possibility if the community decided to be strict about the law and execute Mary by stoning her.

Joseph decided to be gracious and divorce Mary quietly. No sense in adding shame to this already shameful situation, he must have thought. But an angel appeared to Joseph one night in a dream and told him not to be afraid to take Mary as his wife. The angel explained that Mary had conceived a child by the Holy Spirit, that she would give birth to a son (whom they should name Jesus), and that this child would save people from their sins. All of this would take place to fulfill what the prophets had spoken. When Joseph awoke, he did what the angel told him.

Joseph was told to marry an unwed pregnant girl in a culture that harshly stigmatized and sometimes even executed them. People would make assumptions about her lack of virtue and his lack of standards. No respectable man would marry a girl like that. From all appearances, she betrayed him and he didn't make a stand. He could be the laughingstock of the whole town for going through with the wedding. For the rest of his life, he would be misunderstood by many. He looked like a fool.

As for Mary, she not only gave up her reputation; she also gave up her future. Imagine being a teenage girl who, like most teenage girls, dreams about who she will marry, where she will live, and how many kids she might have. Most people have a vision of what they want their future to look like, and Mary was surely no exception. She already knew who she would marry; she probably envisioned a simple and joyful life together with Joseph. But when the angel Gabriel appeared to her and told her what was about to happen, whatever future Mary envisioned was gone. It got erased by the plans of God. Everything she thought she wanted gave way to God's will.

Sure, it was a higher calling, but it would be a difficult one too. The blessing of mothering the Messiah would come at an enormous cost.

How did Mary respond? When Gabriel first appeared to her, she was frightened—or "greatly troubled," as the text says. When Gabriel told her she would have a child, she didn't express doubt or try to negotiate. She only asked how that was possible. And when Gabriel told her that nothing was impossible with God, she simply said, "May it be to me as you have said" (Luke 1:38).

Are you noticing the progression in responses to God? We tend to think that giving our money is a big deal, but it's actually God's training wheels for growing a generous heart. God also asks for us to respond to Him in gratitude with our time, our reputation, and our future. But it doesn't end there. The next person we'll look at in the Christmas story shows us what it's like to give one's whole life to God. Mark 10:45 is a great statement of Jesus' life: "The Son of Man did not come to be served, but to serve, and to give his life as a ransom for many." Jesus came to live a perfect life and offer Himself as the atoning sacrifice that would save those who believe from their sins. He entered human history for one purpose: to make the ultimate sacrifice for us. He gave His very life.

> We tend to think that giving our money is a big deal, but it's actually God's training wheels for growing a generous heart.

That's a level of generosity few of us can comprehend, but it still isn't the highest form of generosity in the Christmas story. The next character we'll look at is God the Father. In the graduate school of generosity, the greatest example to study is the sacrifice God made for us. The hardest thing to give away is whatever is most precious to you. For some of us, that's a dream. For others, it's a mate, or maybe even a child. And that's the sacrifice God made.

Jesus gave His own life, but God gave His own precious Son. Any good parent understands that it's easier to sacrifice your own life than the life of one of your kids. God had nothing more precious that He could offer than Jesus, His only Son.

You'll notice in this progression many of the principles we've discussed in this book. Some in the Christmas story gave their possessions or their time. Others were asked to give much more. All, other than God Himself, gave as a response to God's love, purposes, and calling. Each character gave as an act of worship. And in every case, generosity began with God.

SMART LESSONS FROM THE CHRISTMAS STORY

I would like to leave you with three observations about the Christmas story as it relates to generosity:

1. Generosity is not so much a virtuous act as it is a virtuous response.

If we pat ourselves on the back every time we're generous with our time, money, reputation, or anything else, we'll end up self-righteous. It's really a response of gratitude to God, who was generous with us first.

2. The second observation is one we've already explored— that God measures generosity by the size of the sacrifice.

The magi and shepherds gave something in their worship of Jesus, but not as much as Mary and Joseph did. Giving money and time are like training wheels of generosity compared to the sacrifices made by some.

3. Increasing levels of generosity bring increasing levels of reward and blessing.

The magi and the shepherds got to see the Messiah and tell about Him, but Mary and Joseph got to watch Jesus take His first steps and have heart-to-heart conversations with Him as He grew older. And Jesus' even greater sacrifice resulted in even greater blessing for Him, which we get to share. He paid a price, to be sure, but He did it "for the joy set before him" (Hebrews 12:2). Out of love, He wanted to offer Himself in order to have a relationship with us. And now He sits at the Father's side in glory, where He and the Father wait for the fulfillment of their love and joy at the end of history. Increasing levels of sacrifice bring increasing levels of reward.

If you could stand outside our world and look into it, you would see a stark picture. The world operates on principles of getting and keeping and controlling, with everyone competing against each other for pieces of the pie. But if you look at the incarnation through the lens of generosity, you would have to conclude that the kingdom of God operates on different principles than the world does. "Give, and it will be given to you. A good measure, pressed down, shaken together and running over, will be poured into your lap. For with the measure you use, it will be measured to you" (Luke 6:38). We become small mirrors of the generosity of the King. That's life in the kingdom. That's pure genius. And it can radically change not only your life but also your world.

THE GENIUS LIFE: BISHOP HANNINGTON
How one village found abundance among the ruins

Refugees living in squalor in a war-torn country. Fear, overcrowding, hunger, disease, and death. Appeals being made for generous giving to relieve the suffering. Nothing unusual, right?

But this situation in Uganda was different. One pastor had a vision and a burden for Christians to give from their hearts, not out of duty. He made appeals to the refugees themselves—the believers in the camp—and their response became a model of generosity.

Fighting between insurgents and government forces in Uganda forced thousands of survivors into refugee camps in 2001. Though conditions worsened as the war raged on, nothing could destroy Bishop Hannington Bahemuka's commitment to effective stewardship.

> "Even in this refugee camp," says Hannington, "God had put abundant resources for His work. So I called upon believers to start sharing what they had."

"I had been taught that everything we have belongs to God," says Hannington. "Even in this refugee camp, God had put abundant resources for His work. So I called upon believers to start sharing what they had."

He began to teach about stewardship and led his people in a campaign to give to fellow refugees. They provided blankets to orphans and shared their food, demonstrating love to many who had rarely experienced it. And after two years, it was finally safe to return to their hometown of Bundibugyo.

But when they arrived home, they found that Bundibugyo had been destroyed. Houses, churches, and schools had been torn down. They had to rebuild from scratch.

Instead of asking the typical question—"How can people from the West help us?"—Hannington inspired his people to believe that God had given everything they needed to rebuild and that He would use those who made themselves available to Him.

One by one, people began using their skills and what little they had for the common good. The idea caught on. Mechanics and builders offered their services. One lady donated her only chicken. "We began to rebuild our churches, provided homes and schooling for the orphans, and the needs of the people were met," Hannington says. By using their God-given gifts and the resources they already possessed, a cycle of sustainability was established.

The grace of giving replaced a welfare mentality. Bundibugyo saw the power of an entire community dedicated to generosity. And Hannington is convinced this message can work anywhere because, in one very unlikely place, he and the people of his town witnessed firsthand the transforming power of giving.

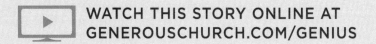 **WATCH THIS STORY ONLINE AT GENEROUSCHURCH.COM/GENIUS**

Chapter 4
DISCUSSION & REFLECTION

The following is a summary of the ideas and questions from Chapter 4. Use them for personal reflection or small group discussion, and consider journaling to record your thoughts and impressions.

BRIGHT IDEAS

Which of these "Bright Ideas" has the most meaning for you? Why?

- God measures generosity not by the size of the gift but by the size of the sacrifice.

- Generosity isn't an act. It's a way of life.

- True generosity doesn't stop with possessions. It starts with them.

IMPACT FROM BISHOP HANNINGTON'S STORY

Do you think most Christians assume that generosity is for the well-off? Why or why not?

How would you respond if, in your deepest time of need, someone challenged you to give?

How did God respond to the generosity of Bundibugyo's believers? In what ways was the mutual generosity of villagers more fulfilling than if they had received large donations from the West?

REFLECTION QUESTIONS

1   Chip said "God measures generosity not by the size of the gift but by the size of the sacrifice." What might "sacrificial" generosity look like for you? Are there any steps you sense God is asking you to take to make your generosity more sacrificial?

2   Read 2 Corinthians 8:2-4. What words or phrase from this passage would you most like to be true about your giving and generosity?

3   The Bible says that God loves a cheerful giver. How would you assess the cheerfulness of your giving? What could you do to help your giving be more of an act of worship?

4   Read James 1:17. As you reflect on your life today, what are you most grateful for?

5   Fast forward to the end of your life. If someone were to write your eulogy and talk about your generosity, what would you hope they would say?

Conclusion

ohn Saville went to be with the Lord a few years ago, and I'm pretty sure I know what he's doing. He's having an extravagant meal with Someone who trusted him with material resources, and they are sharing stories about all the great adventures they had together and about all the fruit they bore. I'm sure he had plenty of friends waiting to see him. Perhaps some of them are saying things like, "Hey, you know that Ingram guy who wrote a check for $200 when my family was living out of our station wagon? I had no idea you were behind that! My kids came to know Christ through that experience." And on and on the line stretches with people waiting to tell John extraordinary stories. Why? Because John was a genius when it came to generosity. He realized he was made for eternity, and he used his worldly wealth to make friends who would welcome him. He demonstrated his genius by investing temporal treasures in things that would last forever. And the returns on his investment continue to grow ... and grow ... and grow.

Learn how to be genius in a small group!

GENIUS DVD FOR SMALL GROUPS

As Chip and John learned, generosity is experienced best alongside others. Launch a small group today, and use the new *Genius* DVD to experience the joy of generosity together as you watch Chip teach about concepts from the book.

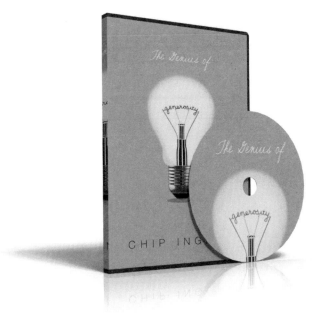

Visit GenerousChurch.com/Genius to order and get started today!

Take Action

TAKE ACTION: THE GENIUS GIVING GROUP

CHIP AND JOHN'S GIVING PARTNERSHIP

In *Genius of Generosity*, Chip and John came together to give to meet the needs of those around them. It was a simple arrangement. John had the money to give and Chip saw needs around him to give to. Then they came together often to enjoy a meal and to celebrate how God was using their generosity to impact others' lives and their own lives as well.

GENIUS GIVING GROUP

Like many parts of our Christian faith (prayer, Bible study, worship) coming together in community often brings a new level of meaning and understanding. God created us to be with others. And giving in partnership with others can bring new levels of understanding of generosity.

That's why we want to challenge you to create a Genius Giving Group over the next four weeks as you continue to read the book.

A Genius Giving Group consists of individuals who pool two things in order to give together to meet these needs and to celebrate the impact of the genius of generosity: a small portion of their resources, and their knowledge of needs around them.

Jesus said "It is more blessed to give than to receive." And a Genius Giving Group is living out this blessed life with others in the context of community.

Perhaps you've done this during Christmas in the past– adopted a needy family and partnered with friends, family, or others within your church to buy gifts and make the holiday a special time through giving. Well, the Genius Giving Group could be viewed similarly—coming together with others to intentionally give to the spiritually or physically needy while you go through the book.

8 EASY STEPS TO CREATE YOUR GROUP

The key to creating an effective Genius Giving Group is found in two commands: keep it simple and set a date. The more simple the group, the more effective it will be. And setting a date produces accountability to get the job done.

There are 8 easy steps to get your Genius Giving Group started:

Step 1
Invite people to be a part of the Genius Giving Group. This could include your family, friends, or small group at church.

Step 2
Brainstorm as a group the possible needs right around you. This might include a single mom, a friend who is having a hard time finding a job, or a family raising money to go on a mission trip. Like Chip and John, try to think of needs within your own backyard ... relationships that you have on a day-to-day basis.

Step 3
Pray together about the needs, and then decide on one or more that you feel like God is calling you to meet.

Step 4

Set a firm date to meet the need(s). Perhaps it could be by the time you finish reading this book in a small group (usually around four weeks). Or if the need is bigger, allow for more time.

Step 5

Each person in the group should decide how much he/she can contribute to meet the need. This may be money. But it also may be time, relationships, or skills and talents.

Step 6

Give together to meet the need! You might want to video the experience to inspire others, if appropriate—see step 8.

Step 7

Celebrate the impact within your group. What lessons did God teach you about the genius of generosity as you gave together? In what ways did you feel challenged? Were there unexpected joys through the experience?

Step 8

Share your story to inspire others! Talk with friends or family about the needs you've supported, or go a step further by sharing your videos with others across the country at GenerousChurch.com/Genius.

Get started with your Genius Giving Group today!

Summary of
BRIGHT IDEAS

 To be smart, spend carefully. To be wise save, regularly. To be genius, give extravagantly.

 Where your money goes, your heart flows.

 Generosity is a gateway into intimacy with God.

 Stewardship is the path. Generosity is the adventure.

 Generous givers make God and His purposes their highest priority.

 Enjoy God's generosity to you ... then share it with others.

Faith increases giving, and giving increases faith.

 Those blessed by God become blessers for God.

 Generous living is joyful living.

 God measures generosity not by the size of the gift but by the size of the sacrifice.

 Generosity isn't an act. It's a way of life.

 True generosity doesn't stop with possessions. It starts with them.

About Chip Ingram

Chip Ingram's passion is to help Christians really live like Christians. As a pastor, author, coach, and teacher for 25 years, Chip has helped people around the world breakout of spiritual ruts to live out God's purpose for their lives. Today, he serves as senior pastor of Venture Church in Los Gatos, California, and president of Living on the Edge—an international teaching and discipleship ministry. He is the author of eleven books, including his newest release, Living on the Edge: Dare to Experience True Spirituality, Overcoming Emotions That Destroy, and Good to Great in God's Eyes. Chip and his wife, Theresa, have four children and eight grandchildren.

GENEROUSCHURCH

As the publisher of *Genius of Generosity* and an initiative of
The National Christian Foundation, GenerousChurch helps
leaders like you release transformational generosity in your
church through leadership development, campaigns, and
culture change. Our books, online learning, coaching, events,
and web resources will help you expand the impact of your
leaders, change your money conversation, and grow
the giving capacity of your people. **Learn more at
GenerousChurch.com.**

 # THE NATIONAL CHRISTIAN FOUNDATION®

National Christian Foundation is a nationwide grantmak-
ing network that funds the Christian causes recommended
by our givers. Using our Giving Fund, you can simplify the
process of giving to your favorite ministries. We can also
help you multiply the impact of your gifts through tax-smart
strategies. Since 1982, NCF has become America's largest
sponsor of donor-advised funds for Christian givers with
over $2.5 billion granted to thousands of ministries for the
glory of God. **Learn more at NationalChristian.com.**

CONTINUE YOUR JOURNEY AT

GenerousYou.com

A great way for you or your group to continue pursuing the genius life is to sign up today for the **free, four-week online learning experience** at GenerousYou.com.

GenerousYou is designed to help you grow in your knowledge and appreciation of the Biblical message of generosity. With four weeks of daily activities, GenerousYou combines the same things you do every day on the web:

- **Read powerful content**

- **Watch inspiring videos**

- **Blog, journal, and share your experience**

Sign up today at GenerousYou.com!

GENEROUSYOU

Explore Drive Introduction Devotional Challenge Contact Login

experience
the life that is truly life

Grow in your understanding of the biblical message
of giving with GenerousYou, a four-week online learning
experience with video, journaling, reading, and more

Get started ○

Reviews: "The 21-Day Giving Challenge was just what I needed to get moving." – Anonymous

Explore

What is GenerousYou?
Learn more, and start
a daily giving routine

Take a test drive

Sample a daily activity
that blends reading,
video, and journaling

Give, and go social

Take our 21-Day Giving
Challenge, and share
your experience

Be inspired, daily

Discover the powerful
Generosify devotional
used in daily activities

Share *Genius* with your entire church!

Are you a pastor or ministry leader looking to raise the tide of generosity in your church or ministry and lead your people to greater spiritual maturity through giving?

Are you a lay leader interested in spreading the message of Biblical generosity and stewardship in your church?

If so, sharing this book with your whole congregation or organization is a wonderful way to get started. Churches across the country, for example, are ordering copies of *Genius of Generosity* to give or sell to their members, in concert with a four-week sermon series and small-group discussions that match the book's outline.

Visit GenerousChurch.com/Genius to order and get started today!

(Customized, private-labeled versions and discounts on large orders are available.)